Caring for elderly people

Caring for elderly people

Understanding and practical help

Susan Hooker, MCSP

Routledge & Kegan Paul

London, Henley and Boston

For my Parents
Charles and Winifred Hope Gill

First published in 1976
by Routledge & Kegan Paul Ltd
39 Store Street,
London WC1E 7DD,
Broadway House,
Newtown Road,
Henley-on-Thames,
Oxon RG9 1EN and
9 Park Street,
Boston, Mass. 02108, USA
Set in IBM Press Roman by
Express Litho Service (Oxford)
and printed in Great Britain by
Redwood Burn Limited, Trowbridge & Esher

ISBN 0 7100 8376 9

Contents

Foreword

It matters not how long we live — but how.

P. J. Bailey
1816–1902

There is no doubt that men and women today are living to a ripe old age. This can be attributed to better environmental conditions, better food and adequate control of the ordinary infections of mankind. The longer we live the more prone we are to suffer from the effects of degeneration of the arteries (strokes), from malfunction of our joints (rheumatism) and from accidents. Very soon we join that dreaded category of 'chronic sick'. Despite the fact that our disability may be chronic, we need not be sick. That is the message of this book. It emphasises the need for, and illustrates the way to, care for the elderly so that they can live a useful and happy life despite a physical or mental handicap.

This excellent book, written by a practising physiotherapist, sets out to inform — to communicate — and this is terribly important in this computer age. It explains the nature of the illness or disability; it deals with the management of the elderly; it gives information about the ancillary and community services that are available to help and inform; and deals in a practical and sympathetic way with the many problems that confront relatives caring for the disabled. It is essential reading for those who look after the elderly and old people themselves will find it interesting and informative.

As a family doctor I can also commend it with confidence to all doctors and nurses. The book is a mine of information and I congratulate the author on her enterprise, her enthusiasm, and her ability to express clearly a message of hope for the elderly and wise counsel for the relatives. A great deal can be done by and for the handicapped. It is not enough to do good; one must do it the right way. That is what this book is all about.

Aberystwyth   John H. Hughes

Preface
and acknowledgments

I think of the elderly as those who find everyday tasks of normal living difficult because various parts of their bodies are becoming less efficient. There is no fixed rate at which people age; different parts of the body wear out at different rates, so the number of years reached is immaterial. Sections of this book may apply to some people in their late sixties and yet the same sections be irrelevant to some in their eighties.

I am concerned here mainly with the elderly who are living independently in their own homes, or with relatives. My aims are to help people understand and cope with the changes that take place, physically and mentally, as one grows older. I hope it will also help elderly people to understand what others are trying to do to enable them to live as fully as possible.

It is only possible to help people in a practical way by understanding *why* they act in a certain way, or *why* they cannot do something that appears quite simple. For this reason I have explained the causes and symptoms of common ailments that are found in old people, and if the basic reason for strange behaviour is kept in mind the enormous amount of help that is offered by relatives will be channelled in a positive direction.

Readers should not confine themselves to the chapter on the disability that primarily concerns them, as they should find suggestions throughout the book which may apply just as readily to them.

I hope this book will also be of use to students of nursing and physiotherapy, and auxiliary nurses who work with the elderly; as well as social workers and other domiciliary helpers. If the elderly are in hospital the role of the relative is taken on by the staff who meet the same physical problems as the relatives, and psychological problems too, except that those arising from family ties are absent. Elderly patients are often completely dependent on the staff who can either make their stay miserable, in which case they react by being obstinate and difficult, or very happy when co-operation from both sides works towards successful rehabilitation and the return home.

I wish to thank Dr John Hughes, MB, BCh, DRCOG for writing the foreword to this book; and my husband for his help and encouragement.

I also wish to thank Dr Gareth Hughes, MB, MRCP, whose running of the Geriatric Unit at Aberystwyth has enabled me to see the results that can be achieved in the rehabilitation of the elderly, and my senior colleague Mrs Laura Jones, MCSP, who has taught me almost all I know about the physiotherapy treatment of old people; her patience, skill and psychological insight have been the basis of this book.

S.H.

1 Normal and abnormal changes

Signs of impending illness

The likelihood of illness is determined to a certain extent by a number of predisposing factors of which most people are basically aware. Heading this list is being overweight. Briefly, obesity is a contributory factor in arthritis, high blood pressure, heart and kidney disease and stroke; it is also closely linked with lack of exercise, inadequate diet and constipation.

People with a chronic cough caused by bronchitis or some other chest disease are susceptible to infection or illness, particularly in the winter and should try to avoid colds. Lack of fluid causing dehydration, and inadequate heating resulting in low body temperature, which are disorders in themselves, also cause illness.

The way an elderly person walks is very informative about his state of health. If the feet are wide apart or the steps shuffling there may be a disorder of the brain causing muscle weakness, and loss of sensation in the soles of the feet; or, if the body is rigid and leaning backwards the balance may be disturbed or the postural reflex upset (see chapter 6).

Lack of care over their appearance, loss of appetite, and insomnia may suggest underlying depression. The frequent desire to pass water may indicate an enlarged prostate gland or a bladder infection. Constipation, diarrhoea and sickness could be a disorder of the digestive system, and excessive fatigue a sign of anaemia, while unusual thirst could be the first symptom of diabetes. Vagueness, sensitivity to cold, and increasing weight combined with loss of appetite are indicative of a decrease in the function of the thyroid gland, which can be controlled. Of course, these are not all the signs that may present themselves; but illness in old age is still illness and changes from the normal pattern of health should be suspect.

Indications of future disability

Most people as they get older become stiffer, slower, and prone to aching joints and weak muscles. Everybody appreciates this but not many will accept that it is happening to them. As the warning signs are noted action must be taken to prevent disability and accidents. This means acknowledging deterioration.

Osteo-arthritis is probably the major discomfort of the elderly, and although pain in the joints tells them clearly that they have it, it is other signs that point to future disability. The feet are placed wider apart than usual and the body sways from side to side in a rolling gait caused by weakness of muscles. The knees tend to 'give way', and muscle weakness gives a feeling of insecurity. Combined with joint stiffness, getting about and rising from a chair become major problems.

Arthritis in the back is often indicated by the hand being held against the small of the back when walking; it means the pain is distracting and causing the balance to be redistributed in an effort to ease it. In fact, it is causing extra strain on the hips and knees which, if not already painful, will become so. Walking on the toes of one foot or keeping the weight on the outer border may be to relieve a bunion or sore heel but will in time upset the balance and irritate arthritis in the knees and hips.

Disturbance of balance or muscle weakness may be manifested by clutching onto furniture while moving about the room. Stretching too far to reach something before moving the feet often results in a fall. This is nearly always accompanied by fear of falling. A burn on a finger from a cigarette, particularly if it is not mentioned, could be due to loss of sensation or bad circulation, the latter also causing very cold hands and feet.

Failing sight is an insidious problem, which may not be noticed by old people, but a friend or relative may see a cup put down inaccurately on a saucer, or a hand fumbling to find the paper or glasses. This leads to accidents caused by tripping over some object on the floor, quite likely causing a fractured hip or wrist. Very often failing sight can be treated by seeing an eye specialist in the early stages, and accidents avoided by taking safety precautions in the home. Deafness, too, is much more likely to be noticed by relatives and if left may also cause accidents, particularly road casualties due to not hearing approaching traffic. About 50 per cent of old people have some impairment in their sense of smell which can be a direct cause of fires and gas poisoning. If possible, gas heating and cooking should be replaced with electricity.

Normal mental changes   The dividing line between normal and abnormal is very vague and depends on terminology and social interpretation. Most people know what is normal behaviour for their relative and should bear this in mind. Many old people are very alert mentally, and this part of ageing may happen only very gradually or not at all. With advancing age there may be changes in an elderly person's behaviour which help him to adapt to the limitations of becoming old rather than allowing it to result in sickness. In modern jargon the word 'disengagement' is used and encompasses the process of withdrawing from situations with which he cannot cope. The speed and range of intellectual performance are reduced, and there is usually lack of spontaneous reaction to unexpected incidents.

Adjustment: learning and experience

The process of adjustment is a continuous one through life, but old age must encompass mental as well as physical change. Intellectual powers are reduced by the inability to absorb new ideas at the same rate; the modern hurried way of life may be overpowering because reactions need to be so quick. The old saying of not being able to teach an old dog new tricks is not true, it just takes longer. The actual performance of tasks and the process of learning are little affected as long as the time allowed is increased. The process of interpreting what is seen and heard is delayed, so in spite of a normal reaction the whole situation is slowed by a delay in the computer. The same principle is applied to inaccuracy of movement and clumsiness; it takes longer to relate an object to its surroundings, for example, an article of clothing may be put on inside out, if the person is in a hurry.

This is one reason why old people do not like things to be changed; they are much less likely to make mistakes if they are in familiar surroundings. Those who have had a spell in hospital and return home with a glowing report of being independent are disappointed and frustrated to find themselves helpless. All the tasks of everyday living they have relearned in hospital cannot be related to the home.

There is no point in hospital staff spending months retraining a person if the relatives have to do everything for him when he gets home. This often occurs through their ignorance of the ex-patient's ability rather than anything else. Many people will walk perfectly with a physiotherapist they are used to, but cannot move at all with a nurse or relative; they do not relate walking with them and are frightened and confused. Relatives should talk to the staff, and under their supervision learn how to help, and act as a bridge between hospital and home.

Inflexibility is common, and causes trouble if it is necessary to live with a son or daughter. The elderly will not find new ways of doing things and do not like their routine upset. It is one of the biggest problems of families living together; the older members do not want to change to fit in with the new life, and the younger ones do not see why they should alter everything to run round them.

Memory

One change in the elderly is gradual loss of memory: not for things that happened years before, but for recent events. The worse the memory the more recent are the events forgotten. Often they will talk about their childhood or the war but cannot remember what happened last week.

Rehabilitation after illness, perhaps a stroke, is made more difficult because instructions are forgotten quickly, and many accidents are caused the same way. When crossing a road they look right then left, but by the time they have looked to see whether there was anything coming from the left they have forgotten if the road was clear to the right. Making decisions, too, can be difficult because of the inability to retain all the necessary facts for a sufficient length of time to come to a rational conclusion.

Personality changes and social behaviour

There are usually changes in personality, but only in that previous traits become more exaggerated. A quiet, nervous person may become shy and frightened of many things, and a rather dominant or touchy person may become demanding or even difficult. These extremes lead to self-absorption and isolation from those around. Irritability and stubbornness are often ways of asserting themselves when they feel unsure and perhaps disregarded.

There are usually changes in depth of conscience, some people's becoming overdeveloped so that they worry about not being independent and being a nuisance to other people. In others conscience is diminished and they become less concerned about other people and their effect on them. They may be less willing to put themselves out, or to try to understand other people, which leads to intolerance and friction.

Deafness

Although very few old people are totally deaf, very many are sufficiently hard of hearing to find life difficult. Deafness comes on very gradually and is often not noticed by the person himself for some time. When he does realise it he should compensate by concentrating extra hard and trying to lip-read a little. Lack of concentration is the reason why someone who is actually capable of picking up a quiet conversation on the other side of the room finds that normally he can hear very little: the common situation of 'hearing when he wants to'.

In most elderly people there is no definite change in the ear, but the nerves become less efficient. They are unable to distinguish consonants and, if shouted at, the vowel sounds become blurred as well. They can hear low notes better than high ones so can converse more easily with a man than a woman. The way to talk most easily with a deaf person is to sit near them and speak in a *normal* voice close to their ear.

Deaf people can become withdrawn through lack of contact and sometimes suffer from hallucinations or become paranoid and think everyone is talking about them. A great deal of patience is required to maintain normality, and to treat deaf people as if they, too, are normal.

Extra care must be taken in the house and also particularly on the road; many accidents are caused by a deaf person not hearing approaching traffic. The normal form of deafness experienced by the elderly is usually greatly helped by the use of a hearing aid, though many have them and then refuse to wear them, but I think this is often because they may not be fitted properly or the person has not been given adequate instruction on their use.

At the first sign of deafness the doctor should be consulted; possibly all that is required is to have the ears washed out. If further treatment is necessary he will refer the patient to the local clinic where the ears will be examined and the degree of deafness assessed. Hearing aids and batteries are issued as free loans for as long as they are required and will be properly fitted and the user shown how they work. If, after a few days it obviously is not comfortable or the volume cannot be maintained, an appointment should be made to go back to the clinic. It is quite pointless having an aid that does not improve the hearing. Many people are put off by the old-fashioned type that is so conspicuous it announces to all the world that the wearer is deaf, but these are now being replaced by the small compact type which fits behind the ear; on a man it is hardly noticed, and on a woman it is hidden completely by the hair.

One strong word of warning about buying a hearing aid. If you decide to buy one instead of using a National Health one, go to a reputable firm. I have known more than one old lady who has handed over up to £90 for an aid to a persuasive door-to-door salesman. Some are very good at convincing the buyer how good their model is, and even make them believe they need it when they do not; so be warned.

Loss of sight
Gradual dimming of vision is a normal part of becoming old which is often not noticed for a while. The eyes become long-sighted towards middle age due to distortion in the shape of the eyeball and loss of elasticity of the lens. In old age further changes take place and the eyes are subject to a variety of diseases.

As soon as an impairment is noticed go to the doctor; possibly it is only a matter of changing the glasses but more likely an appointment will be made to see the eye specialist at the hospital.

Loss of sight causes similar psychological difficulties to deafness in that sufferers sometimes become timid and shy, feeling unable to keep up a conversation, or they may become paranoid and withdrawn or suffer from hallucinations. Lack of confidence is a great problem and one that is bound to crop up as life becomes restricted, particularly as far as getting around is concerned. The situation can be helped a great deal by making sure that everything is always kept in the same place to make moving about and finding things as simple as possible. Familiarity, combined with acquiring a 'sixth sense' can make many people almost independent.

Lack of contact with people is felt deeply, but this can be re-established by touch. When talking to someone who cannot see very well it helps to touch their arm or hand. If there are several people present say the name of the person being addressed so the blind member of the group is not left wondering whether he should be answering or not.

Safety in the home must be organised carefully to eliminate accidents. One change in vision is the inability to adapt quickly from light to dark and *vice versa*, so all dark corners should be well lit to avoid a sudden change in light intensity. All small mats should be removed and the floors left unpolished (see 'Common sense and precautions' and 'Safety aids' in chapter 16).

Care and understanding by relatives

On the whole, harmony in a household is dependent on the younger members. I have tried to explain changes which can take place and cause the elderly to behave in ways that can be trying. But, although understanding and tolerance are essential and will make difficulties seem less important, there is a danger of allowing an elderly person to rule the roost and have everyone running round. To allow the young ones to lead their lives fully it is necessary for the elderly to conform basically to their way of life, and to be stimulated into retaining their independence and interest in life around them. The trouble is, it is natural for the elderly to withdraw gradually from those things they feel unable to do and limit their lives to their immediate surroundings. Somehow a balance must be sought between bullying them into reluctant activity and allowing unacceptable withdrawal.

Mental and physical health are closely connected and affect each other greatly, and if an old person is unhappy he or she will nearly always succumb to physical illness as well. Loneliness is not necessarily eliminated by being in a family. Relatives can do much to help the elderly feel part of the family, encouraging them to take part in discussions and in decisions if possible, and to do useful household jobs. The response will be much more positive if they are asked to peel the potatoes because the daughter is putting the baby to bed, than if they are told it is good for them to help. Just making the elderly feel needed and useful encourages a healthy outlook and keeps them going. Never mind if they do not do a job 'your' way. Let them get on with it.

Many old people will not accept that they are unable to do things; they will not seek help because it means admitting they are old and failing, and this attitude is one that causes much disablement. One of the reasons for writing this book is to encourage people to get the right help at the right time. An elderly person should not turn away well-meant offers of help from neighbours for fear of losing 'independence'. If neighbours feel snubbed they may be less likely to offer again when help is really needed. As I have explained, old people need longer to do things and this must be remembered all the time. If they feel they are being hurried, or are being a nuisance because they are holding things up they often go quite blank and incapable of doing anything, a reaction that is usually interpreted as stubbornness or lack of co-operation. The same reaction may occur if they are faced with an unfamiliar situation. I am sure most people have experiences which create this blankness; for some it is examinations, for others walking into a crowded room.

Many old people need constant encouragement to maintain their normal standard of physical and mental activity. Bullying often results in stubbornness, but enthusiasm conveyed from one person to another is the most effective form of stimulation.

Young relatives and all other members of a family can be a great help in preventing depression and illness after bereavement. Of course, grief must be allowed to run its time and serve its purpose, but if prolonged and deep it may turn into mental illness. A watch should be kept on the diet too, particularly if living alone; many bereaved people do not bother to eat, and live in a disordered fashion, perhaps staying in bed all day, or sleeping on and off in an armchair instead of going to bed normally.

Danger times for the elderly are when they are under stress, for example, if they have to move to another house, particularly in cities with new development plans. Help, support and understanding at these times not only makes them feel less unhappy but prevents the sequel of illness or depression.

Old people need others to care about them; in my experience they will put up with all manner of discomfort, pain and unhappiness if they feel someone *cares* that they are in pain or unhappy or uncomfortable. It is a matter of understanding, the sort of *caring* understanding that is the foundation of a happy family unit.

Attitudes of relatives

Discord in a multi-generation family is not necessarily the fault of the old ones alone. The younger generations are often to blame for disablement in the elderly for two reasons: 'over-caring' and 'not-caring'. The 'not-caring' group are usually fairly easily explained; they take in mother or mother-in-law because they feel it is their duty, without any real knowledge of or liking for her. She creates more work, possibly interferes, and is generally difficult, and the problems that were abstract when the decision was made become very real indeed. At the first bout of illness she is put to bed, but the time somehow never comes when she is well enough to get up again. Fairly soon she is bedfast and a heavy nursing problem who ends up in hospital.

The 'over-caring' group nearly kill their beloved spouse or parent, and sometimes themselves, with kindness. They live together in harmony and companionship, the one 'looking after' the other. He or she waits on the other hand and foot, and it is not long before it becomes expected. The old one takes less exercise than ever before, probably eats too much and in time becomes obese, stiff and immobile.

I have illustrated the extremes, and of course, there are many degrees in between, but they are by no means all that exceptional. It is hard to be kind and patient and loving to someone you do not care for very much, and it is hard to watch one's own dear mother struggling to put her own stockings on, but it must be done. If it is not, the 'over-caring' way or the 'not-caring' way will end in disability in the elderly and exhaustion and depression in the young.

The balance must be found where the old person is doing everything for him- or herself (and others for that matter), that he or she possibly can. The elderly should not be helped unless it is really necessary, but on the other hand they should not be ignored when they do need help. If the balance is right the elderly will do their utmost to be independent, but if they do not have to bother why should they? If they know they are struggling to do things of which they are incapable, they give up, and why shouldn't they? Balance of help and caring is the key to successful cohabitation of young and old (see chapter 12).

2 Arthritis

There are basically two major types of arthritis; osteo-arthritis and rheumatoid arthritis, but even though they can both be incapacitating, they are clinically very different. It is important to know the differences between them as they need very different management medically, and a different approach psychologically by the sufferer and those around.

Osteo-arthritis

Causes and symptoms

Osteo-arthritis is by far the more common. Most people of advanced middle age are affected to some degree. Many are oblivious of it until they have a fall or some other injury which starts up inflammatory processes in a joint.

One of the major resulting symptoms of an arthritic joint is weakness and spasm of the muscles around the joint. The spasm tries to protect the joint from movement and so prevent pain, but in fact causes fatigue and more pain. The weakness can add another hazard by making the joint unstable and liable to 'give way'.

Broadly speaking, osteo-arthritis is the wearing out of the joint. This happens when a disturbance of the mechanics of the joint causes weight to be unevenly distributed on the joint surfaces, and puts an abnormal strain on them. Some occupations predispose towards osteo-arthritis by requiring continual use of one joint or a combination of joints; for example, miners and dockers often get painful backs, or factory workers doing repetitive work involving their hands develop painful thumbs or fingers.

The majority of arthritic joints are backs, hips, and knees; all weight-bearing joints which are subjected to a great deal of hard work in their lifetime. People with arthritis are often overweight which puts even more strain on the joints (see chapter 9).

The main troublesome symptoms are pain, muscle weakness, and deformity. The condition cannot be cured but relief of symptoms is possible.

Pain

The most distressing symptom is pain, which largely causes the other two. Although pain may vary considerably it is rarely absent. The pattern of arthritis tends to be one of 'flare ups' and remissions related very closely, if I dare say it, to the weather. In my experience it has a direct effect upon pain and stiffness; there seems to be some factor other than temperature involved because patients in a regulated hospital atmosphere can tell whether there has been a frost or not, and whether it will rain the next day, and they are very rarely wrong; so it is not such an old wives' tale as some people suppose. There is one point to make concerning arthritic pain; if one is suffering from arthritis of the hip it would seem reasonable to expect the pain to be in the hip, and it is, but it is quite likely to be down the front of the thigh as well, and even in the knee. This is because the skin and muscles of the front of the thigh are supplied by the same nerves as the hip joint, and sometimes the pain impulses relayed to the brain from the hip are misinterpreted as coming from the thigh. The same thing may occur in any joint, particularly those of the back, when pain is felt down the leg or round the chest (see 'Sciatica' in chapter 2) or the shoulder where any injury to the shoulder joint is manifest by pain in the upper part of the outside of the arm, and not in the actual joint as would be expected.

The conservative treatment for osteo-arthritic pain is heat to increase the blood supply and to take away residual waste products, which are a source of pain in themselves, and analgesic or pain-killing drugs prescribed by the doctor.

There are two groups of massage creams that, even though they will not cure, are most effective; one contains an analgesic, which reduces superficial pain directly but will not affect the actual joint. The other works by counter-irritation; this group causes a burning sensation on the skin which transfers the concentration from the pain in the joint to the uncomfortable skin, and in doing so breaks down the obsessive connection between the brain and the joint pain. It also increases the blood flow in the muscles which reduces the pain caused by muscle spasm. Although the latter type sounds very clever the former is the more effective; and the result achieved by both is supplemented by the actual rubbing involved in applying the cream.

Heat is a great source of comfort to arthritic joints but many elderly people have slightly impaired sensation in their skin, so the application of heat should be supervised. It is more beneficial if it is comfortably warm rather than very hot, because if the heat itself causes discomfort more muscle spasm will result. Also, it is easy to burn the skin if sensation is not normal and a constant watch should be kept to see that the skin is not becoming red and mottled with over-heating. Many old people who cannot feel normally think that the heat is not enough and therefore move nearer to it, and end up with a burn.

Infra-red or radiant heat are the standard forms of heat that are most easily used in the home, and are applied by sitting in front of an electric fire (with a guard around it). No area should be exposed for more than fifteen minutes at a stretch, and the heat should be three feet away and at a right angle to the part to be treated. A sun-lamp is not a suitable treatment for arthritis and used by a layman can cause serious burns.

A hot water bottle wrapped in a towel or with a good cover on it is a useful way to warm awkward areas such as the back of the neck. Heat can be applied to the small of the back by sitting in an upright garden chair, the canvas type with a gap at the bottom of the back.

Wax is used a great deal in hospitals for arthritis of the hands and feet, and can quite easily be used at home. It can be bought in blocks from any big chemist's and should be melted slowly in a large pan or bowl on the stove; the edge of an Aga is ideal. If it is melted too quickly it is too hot to use. Always test the heat with one finger before plunging the whole hand in; it should feel comfortably warm and leave a coat of wax on it which rapidly turns white as it is taken out of the bowl. Before starting, a towel and a plastic bag should be placed within reach. Place one hand at a time into the wax and lift it straight out, wait a few seconds for the wax to dry and turn white and then dip it quickly in again. It should not be left in because the previous layer will just be melted off instead of a new one being put on. Dip the hand in six times in succession, and put it in a plastic bag and wrap the towel round it to keep the warmth in. If necessary repeat with the other hand and then sit back and enjoy the warmth for twenty minutes. After that time take off the towel and the bag and the wax will peel off like a glove. One warning when using wax; if it is spilt on clothes it is almost impossible to get off.

Heat is not a treatment in itself, but should be used in conjunction with exercises. The warmth reduces pain and relaxes muscles, enabling fuller movement to be performed. When exercising the hands after using wax, the wax that has been peeled off is a useful pliable ball which is excellent for strengthening and dexterity exercises. It can be pinched, rolled, moulded and squeezed before being put back into the pot to melt down again for the next day.

Muscle weakness   This accompanies any injured or inflamed joint, wasting the substance of the muscles surrounding and supporting it. The lack of support results in strain and further injury to the joint, so setting up a vicious circle.

Having applied heat by one of the methods mentioned above, the exercises set out in chapter 14 should be followed. It is far more important to do a few accurately than dozens wrongly, and it is more difficult to do them correctly than one would imagine, so they should be studied carefully. Start with a few, and gradually increase the number each day as the muscles gain strength.

Deformity   This has frightening implications and conjures up visions of cripples and hunchbacks, but in fact all it means, in this context, is stiffening of a joint to such a degree that the normal range of movement cannot be maintained and is therefore restricting enough to cause disability. Sufferers of both types of arthritis may reach a stage when inflammation becomes acute and continues over a long time and all the surrounding fibrous tissue of ligaments and capsule become involved. The pain and weakness in the muscles prevent the joint being used fully, and very quickly it will be quite unable to move properly. The knee is a good example; when the sufferer finds how comfortable it is with a cushion under the knees it is not long before they will not go quite straight again. The locking mechanism of the knee which relies on the ability to be fully extended to make it firm and stable is lost, and we are back to the problem of 'giving way'. The same effect can be gained by too much sitting in a chair, the knees become bent, and the hips too, making the person assume a chair-shaped deformity.

Chair-shaped deformity

The acute pain suffered by arthritics is usually caused by movement at extremes of range, that is, fully bent or fully straight. These extreme movements are painful due to the ligaments and joint capsule being inflamed and shortened, but it is necessary to keep them in their lengthened state to prevent permanent deformity. The knees must be straightened right out so the back of the legs meet the bed, and then bent so the heel almost meets the seat. These movements may well cause pain which must be put up with to a certain extent; they should be performed by the muscles and not by an enthusiastic helper who may push too far and set up inflammation and pain, which will make the deformity worse (see chapter 14).

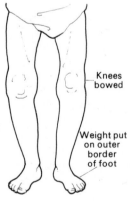

Knees bowed

Weight put on outer border of foot

Osteo-arthritis in the knees

The amount of pain that should be tolerated depends on the condition of the joint. If it is hot and swollen the inflammation will be increased by vigorous exercise, and could be caused by it, in which case the exercises should be moderated accordingly or even stopped for a day or two, except the one which tightens up the thigh muscles while the leg is straight. This one cannot do any harm but will prevent deterioration.

Being aware that bad postural habits can lead to deformity is a great help in being able to prevent them. The limbs should

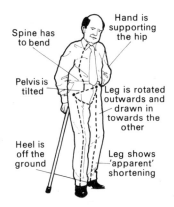

Spine has to bend

Hand is supporting the hip

Pelvis is tilted

Leg is rotated outwards and drawn in towards the other

Heel is off the ground

Leg shows 'apparent' shortening

Typical posture of a man with osteo-arthritis of the hip

be positioned so as to discourage deformity, and movements performed in the opposite direction. For example, if the leg rolls outwards from the hip it should be rolled in to touch the other one with the toes, and if the knees become stiff the appropriate exercises should be begun straight away to counteract it (see chapter 14).

Treatment   In nearly all cases arthritis comes on fairly gradually, and if there is awareness of what is happening a great deal can be done to prevent it getting very much worse, and to keep the pain under control. There is no point in letting it progress and philosophically attributing it to 'old age'. As I stress in chapter 3 (Stroke) nobody else can make the legs move but the person concerned; it is common to find people in hospital who think the doctors and physiotherapists are going to 'cure' their arthritis; it has to be explained that although help can be given no one else can actually carry out the exercises necessary.

It is important to keep the weight down (see chapter 9). If the joints have to carry around an extra stone or two they will wear out even quicker. The strain taken by a joint during a step is four times the body weight, so the weakened muscles, too, will have to work much harder. It is also very important to keep the joints, and indeed the whole body, moving. Lack of movement is the main cause of pain and stiffness leading to deformity; therefore, unless an old person is really unwell it is not wise for him to stay in bed. He will be comfortable there but after a few days will be so stiff that getting up will require such effort and create such pain that he may refuse to do so. One lady I know to whom this happened stayed in bed for ten years. So it is important to encourage mobility by getting up from the chair occasionally and walking around a little, perhaps to make a cup of tea, or do some dusting, or to go and see how the garden is coming along, if there is one. Short excursions fairly frequently are much better than one long one and are far less exhausting.

Standing still is not good for arthritics as the weight has to be maintained on painful joints and they become stiff and sore. It is easy to arrange to sit down to wash up, peel the vegetables or do the ironing. While waiting for a bus keep marking time to prevent the joints becoming stiff. Many people are very stiff in the morning and take a long time to get going, but practising some exercises in bed before attempting to get up is a great help.

To summarise a few 'dos' and 'don'ts':

Don't stay in bed unless it is absolutely necessary.
Don't put pillow under knees.
Don't sit with the legs crossed.
Don't stand when you can sit.
Don't stay in one position for too long.

Do make sure the joint is moving *fully*.
Do keep the muscles working *strongly*.
Do *keep moving* about.

See chapters 13, 14 and 16.

Rheumatoid arthritis

Causes and symptoms

Rheumatoid arthritis is a chronic disease involving many joints over an extended number of years, and is accompanied by various general disturbances. Women are affected about three times as often as men, and although no age group is exempt it is most commonly found in the thirties to fifties. There is no proof that it is hereditary but there is often a history of the disease in the family.

The onset is usually insidious, beginning with aching in the joints, muscle stiffness and a general feeling of being unwell; headache, unusual tiredness, loss of weight and often a persistent low temperature. The small joints of the hands and feet are usually affected first of all, and gradually the larger ones, elbows, shoulders, ankles and knees; the hips are not usually involved. In a few cases the onset is sudden with acute pain in many joints from the beginning.

The joints are swollen and painful as their internal structures become inflamed and thickened. The articular surfaces are damaged making movement stiff and painful. The muscles around each joint also become involved, because pain is caused during movement and the limbs are held rigidly with the muscles in spasm in an effort to protect the joints. The lack of use causes weakness and wasting of the muscle bulk.

In the early stages the damage caused to the joints can be reversed if the disease is arrested. It is an illness of acute 'flare-ups' and chronic stages, each 'flare-up' leaving more damage until the point is reached where the joints are irretrievably altered. The ligaments and the fibrous capsule round the joint also become inflamed and sticky adhesions are formed which contract as scar tissue. The combination of this contracture with weakness of the muscles, which would normally support the joint, results in the distinctive alterations easily recognisable in an arthritic sufferer, such as the typical side flexion of the wrist and the deviation of the fingers.

Each joint adopts its own characteristic deformity. Given time the adhesions harden and the deformities become permanent, this is why it is so important to manage the disease correctly. Permanent deformity means permanent disability.

The pain and disability caused by rheumatoid joints are accompanied by various general changes such as anaemia and other disturbances of the blood's constituents. The bone ends adjacent to the affected joints become brittle and lose some of the calcium content, which in advanced cases is laid down in the ligaments and tissues of the actual joint, and forms a bony union. The skin very often becomes papery and little nodules of hard matter are formed under the skin, usually of the finger joints and along the back of the forearms and elbows. In a few people the eyes become very inflamed and sore.

Outcome   At the onset of this disease it is impossible to say how quickly or how far it will progress. The severity of the 'flare-ups' and the length of the remissions vary in every case but they are indicative of the degree of severity and duration of the disease. Those who have very acute phases fairly often have a poorer outcome than those whose 'flare-ups' have longer gaps between them.

There are three phases through which the affected joints will pass. During the early stages the inflammation of the tissues subsides and the structures involved return to normal leaving no permanent changes in the joints. The inflammation of subsequent 'flare-ups' produces changes which cannot be reversed; any damage caused at this time is permanent. The final development is that of permanent deformity when the joints become almost incapable of any movement. At any time the inflammation may burn itself out, arresting the disability at that point.

The pain which accompanies rheumatoid arthritis is present almost all the time, but is very acute during a 'flare-up' and subsides to a continuous ache during remissions. There seems to be a quality in the pain caused by this type of arthritis which makes the victims very depressed, and unwillingness to move is often due as much to this as to the actual pain they know it will cause; added to this is the fact that they feel unwell almost all the time, which lowers the resistance to pain and makes coping with the situation much more difficult for them. Anyone in contact with a person with rheumatoid arthritis should bear this in mind because there is a hopeless-ness and stubbornness present which can be very difficult to understand and be patient with. On the other hand some suf-ferers never cease to amaze with their cheerfulness and forti-tude, but the older they get the more difficult it is to keep this up.

Treatment

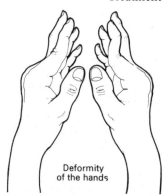

Deformity
of the hands

A typical case of rheumatoid
arthritis

In the acute stage rest and a good diet combined with treat-ment from the doctor are the main considerations. Changes in ankles, knees, elbows and other joints can be discouraged by maintaining the limbs in normal positions; that is, by not putting a pillow under the knees, even if it is more comfort-able, and by keeping the arms stretched out by the sides rather than folded across the front of the body.

The bed should be firm but have a soft mattress as the skin is thin and liable to break down into bed sores. The position-ing of the limbs must incorporate relief of pressure areas to prevent friction on the skin (see chapter 11).

If only one joint 'flares up' rest may be achieved more satisfactorily by sitting in a chair with the limb supported (see chapter 13). Muscles should be tightened statically, that is, without moving the joint, as lads do to show off the muscles in their arms. Tightening in this way maintains the use of the muscles until the joints may be moved; it also helps to prevent deformity (see chapter 14, 2, Knees: a, 1).

After the initial inflammation has subsided the limbs may be moved very gently with the help of a physiotherapist; this should not be done by relatives as it is easy to damage the joint even further. Very few people who have had a 'flare up' will not be having professional treatment to increase move-ment of the joints gradually. At first only a little movement will be achieved and must not cause excessive pain. Pain is caused by inflammation so increased pain means increased damage to the joint.

After the very acute stage the inflammation will subside, though it will still be active. The joints will be less swollen and painful and allow more movement, though the pain-inflammation cycle is still active. Throughout the disease it is the yardstick by which progress or regression is measured.

The movement of the joints can be gradually increased, and the muscles strengthened by more active contraction. In spite of the static tightening exercises the muscles will have lost quite a lot of power, and some deformity will probably be evident. This is the time to prevent permanent deformity by moving the joints through as full a range as the pain permits.

When the doctor allows it, the elderly person may begin walking again. It will be a painful and slow procedure and many people find it frightening after several inactive weeks. Some elderly people who have had rheumatoid arthritis for many years become experienced in managing their own condition and know when movement can begin or walking started again.

Throughout the phases of this disease the initiative must be taken by the doctor and physiotherapist; an over-eager and helpful relative can do a great deal of harm in a very short time, though after some years the person is usually able to guide them by the feel of the joints. The best way for relatives to help is by talking to the physiotherapist and finding out how much can be done, and by being as patient and understanding as possible. For the home based, professional guidance is essential.

Many old people with this disease may be in the burnt-out stage with residual deformity and its disabilities, or it may run along in a sub-acute stage for several months. Thought must be given to aids and gadgets and possible alterations to the home.

Returning home   Adjusting to home life after a spell in hospital can be difficult (see chapter 1). The person will probably not be as mobile as before but the full and correct use of alterations and gadgets can often make even a severely handicapped person independent. The family should support and encourage independence, not rush to take over everything. It may take the family much effort to get the aids together, but it is important for the psychological and physical health of the elderly person that he or she feels able to continue with a role in the family and community.

Bring the bed downstairs, and put rails up by the bath, lavatory, and all steps (see chapter 15). A chair must be made the correct height and if necessary one with a tip-up seat can be used to take most of the struggle out of getting up. The deformity and weakness of the hands is a great source of frustration but there are aids for practically every normal activity to make life easier. Each individual must decide which are suitable and necessary; general advice cannot be offered here as each deformity is slightly different and is coped with in various ways with differing degrees of success (see chapter 16).

Exercises should be performed twice a day, every day, to prevent weakness and deformity from becoming incapacitating (see chapter 14). Many people lose heart and become depressed with the endless struggle but encouragement from relatives can be an enormous help.

Arthritis in the shoulder This acutely painful condition (which is not rheumatoid arthritis) seems to come for no reason and becomes very severe after a few weeks. The pain is felt first in the arm just below the shoulder joint. It becomes stiff and aching. Later, the pain radiates down the arm to the thumb and first finger and is even present when the arm is at rest. It interferes with sleep and the side of the painful arm cannot be lain on. Pain and loss of sleep often cause depression. The muscles round the joint are in spasm and there may be slight swelling; the arm is held close to the body to inhibit movement which in time causes weakness of the muscles surrounding the joint. It is usually present for many months, and sometimes as long as two years, and although many treatments are tried in that time it clears up spontaneously in the end.

When the pain is very acute, rest is the only answer. Active movement increases the inflammation. The arm can be supported with a sling but this should be taken off at intervals and the arm moved away from the body if possible. Prolonged inactivity causes adhesions in the joint and prevents movement after the inflammation subsides.

After the first very painful stage has worn off, some movement should be attempted, but without causing too much pain; a few minutes three times a day should be spent trying to improve the range.

As the pain recedes and is absent at night more extensive exercises can begin to return the joint to full movement and strengthen the muscles. The best way to start is to sit on a chair with the arm hanging by the side and holding a small weight in the hand to put slight traction on the joint. Swing the arm forwards and back and round in circles paying attention to the backward and outward movement. The arm must be raised over the head, which is most easily carried out lying on a bed.

Most people have so much pain initially that they see a doctor who will prescribe pain-relieving drugs and probably suggest a course of physiotherapy later on. 'Deep heat' is helpful in increasing the circulation to the joint and relaxing the muscles enabling movement to be carried out more freely.

An effort is required to use the arm fully as it recovers to strengthen the arm and mobilise the joint so it can work normally and painlessly from then on; if adhesions remain, so will the pain.

Sciatica

Causes 'Sciatica' is a symptom of a disorder in the lower back, or inflammation of the sciatic nerve which runs down the back of the leg to the ankle and foot. Pain is usually caused by pressure on, or irritation of, the nerve as it comes out of the spinal cord and backbone, or vertebral column; but the pain is felt in areas of skin and muscles supplied by the nerve rather than in the back. The greater the pressure on the nerve the further down the leg the pain will be felt. It is a common ailment among the elderly, but from casual observation seems to affect men more than women.

Almost all elderly people have some osteo-arthritis in the small joints between the bones of the vertebral column, and this, combined with a narrowing of the discs, reduces the spaces between the bones and narrows the openings through which the nerves leave the spinal cord. The nerves either become pinched when certain movements are performed or become inflamed due to constant irritation as they pass through the narrowed openings.

The shock absorbing properties of the discs are also less efficient as they become thinner and allow the vertebrae to knock against one another. The effect is to produce typical osteo-arthritic symptoms which include spurs of bone being thrown out from the main bodies. These spurs often touch a nerve, or, during certain movements, pinch a nerve causing acute pain, which presents a picture similar to a 'slipped disc'. In some severe cases spurs from two vertebrae may join up and make the joint between them immobile, either relieving the pain by limiting the movement, or making it acute and permanent. Unfortunately little can be done without an operation which is not suitable for elderly people.

Due to man's upright position the intervertebral discs take an enormous amount of weight, and as each step is taken they must cushion the vibration which would otherwise be transmitted to the spinal cord. This causes the discs to become thinner, lose their shock-absorbency, and be liable to crack or 'slip'.

A disc is made up of two parts, making it liable to two different types of injury. Basically, it is formed of fibrous material shaped into a hard ring, in the centre of which is a gelatinous pulpy substance. If the ring cracks the pulpy substance oozes out and comes to rest on the nerve as it passes out of the spinal cord. If the ring breaks in two places a section of it may pop out and hit the nerve. Although the symptoms are similar in both cases the mode of onset will tell a doctor or physiotherapist which type of injury has been sustained, which will affect the treatment given.

The pulpy centre oozes out gradually and symptoms appear some time after the injury, usually beginning with stiffness in the back which slowly becomes more painful and spreads down the leg. When the ring breaks and a piece pops out the familiar story of bending down, feeling acute pain in the back and being unable to straighten up again is related. The back cannot be straightened because a piece of disc causes a mechanical block, making it impossible to regain the upright position. Unlike straightforward arthritis the pain is only felt on some movements, usually on bending to one side and either bending forwards or backwards.

'Sciatica' can also be caused by a bone in the back moving slightly from its normal position. This is not very common but can occur during a fall and may affect one of two sites; either, one vertebra will slip on another so that the two become out of line and cause the nerve to be stretched round the displaced bone, or the sacro-iliac joint formed between the triangular bone, or sacrum, at the base of the spine and the main pelvic bone becomes dislocated so that the two do not interlock correctly. In both cases the symptoms follow the pattern of pain and 'sciatica' due to pressure on the nerve.

The last cause of 'sciatica', which is rarely seen, is inflammation of the nerve itself due to a virus infection or a direct injury such as a knock which bruises the tissue of the nerve. The pain in the leg is acute, but there are usually no symptoms in the back, and it often clears up as the virus subsides or the bruise is reabsorbed.

Accompanying all the above symptoms is spasm of the muscles in the back which creates increased fatigue and further narrowing of the disc spaces. Depression and loss of sleep are common due to the constant pain, discomfort and restrictions imposed by limited movement and the inability to get comfortable.

The neck can be affected in a similar way, except that the pain is felt in the arm or in the shoulder blade area.

Treatment   Constant pressure will in time cause numbness and pins and needles of the skin of the leg, and weakness of the muscles supplied by the sciatic nerve, which are those of the back of the thigh, the front of the lower leg, and calf and the small muscles of the foot. The main treatment is to release pressure from the nerve itself by manual or mechanical traction to the spine, but this is not suitable for many old people, though the neck can often be treated very successfully by this method. 'Deep heat' in the form of short wave diathermy helps in reducing the spasm that causes aching in the muscles. If the muscles can be relaxed the pressure is sometimes released spontaneously.

In most cases expert diagnosis is necessary and specialised treatment important. It is not a complaint to be taken lightly or shrugged off and treated at home. Avoid activities and positions that increase the pain. The degree of pain in the leg is an indication of the pressure being put on the nerve. It usually helps to make the bed harder by putting boards or an old door under the mattress, and most people are more comfortable in an upright rather than a low chair. If a stick is used it must be the right height (see p. 150) and it must have a rubber ferrule on the bottom of it to prevent it slipping.

3 Stroke

A stroke is the disability caused by one of three circulatory disturbances in the brain; showing weakness of one side of the body (hemiplegia), speech and sensation disturbances, and some emotional or psychological changes. First, an artery may become hardened and thin, and liable to burst under stress; high blood pressure, unaccustomed exercise, or even a strong cough or sneeze can create enough pressure within the artery to break the wall and cause a haemorrhage into the brain tissue destroying the nerve cells of which it is made.

Second, the hardened walls of the arteries become rough and narrowed, and collect particles from the blood as it flows, forming a clot which is attached to the side of the artery. The clot slows the flow of blood to the brain, sometimes stopping it altogether; the part of the brain deprived of its blood supply dies, destroying the nerve cells. This type of stroke is called a cerebral (brain) thrombosis (clot).

The third type is similar in effect, but is more common in people who already have heart disease. A clot of blood forms in the heart and breaks away, travelling in the blood stream until it reaches one of the narrowed blood vessels of the brain which it cannot pass through, and so acts as a plug stopping any further blood flow to that section of the brain, which consequently dies.

The extent of the damage caused by these disturbances decides the ultimate disability that will remain. In a minor stroke the damage is small and often reversible. The type of stroke caused by a cerebral haemorrhage may appear to be very serious at the outset, but the blood forms into a clot and is gradually reabsorbed into the system. Some nerve cells will have been killed and can never be replaced, but many will only have been bruised and will recover to function normally.

A major stroke is more often the result of a clot, because the part of the brain that dies through lack of blood can never be regenerated, though massive haemorrhages can leave a great deal of damage even after reabsorption.

It is usual for only one side of the brain to be affected, the blood vessels supplying the brain being bilateral. The nerves coming from the brain cross over to supply the limbs of the opposite side of the body.

Onset In most cases there is some warning of the onset of a stroke, usually giddiness, nausea or blurred vision, before a tingling sensation down one side of the body. In some cases consciousness is lost. If the stroke occurs during sleep the first indication is the inability to get out of bed and possibly to call for help, or the noisy, deep breathing may attract attention.

The first symptoms that are noticed are weakness or paralysis of one arm and leg; speech may be absent or slurred and sensation altered or entirely absent. Immediately after the attack the arm and leg are usually quite floppy or flaccid, and gradually as the shock wears off, a little movement may return. In major strokes the flaccidity may last some weeks and indeed never recover, or is replaced by spasticity of certain groups of muscles creating the typical posture of the stroke victim.

Loss of speech is common and occurs when the speech-controlling centre in the brain is damaged. In many cases it returns spontaneously in a few days but other people have a long period of difficulty, and some never regain their speech.

Alterations in sensation are usual; for some the skin becomes over-sensitive, temperatures feel extreme and slight pressure very painful. More commonly sensation becomes reduced, and may be accompanied by numbness and pins and needles. In some people all sensation is lost including joint sense which tells us the position of the limbs, and for them the limbs feel as if they do not exist.

The time spent in bed depends on the doctor in charge, and whether or not consciousness has been lost; if it has, admission to hospital is usual. Most people who have remained conscious throughout are allowed up after a few days.

Mental attitude   Among illnesses of the elderly the stroke is one of the most common, and one that causes fear and despondency. It usually comes out of the blue and is a terrible shock to the elderly person and the relatives. Immediately, the question arises as to how much damage has been done and it is usually assumed that it will cause permanent disability and make the victim an invalid. Obviously, a catastrophe of this sort in any family is very distressing, but the fear of the possible consequence is due to lack of knowledge about what can be done to help people in this situation.

Mental attitude is vitally important. Many stroke sufferers feel that suddenly their active life is ended, and become depressed, and refuse to have anything to do with the weak side of the body; in some cases they will not even look at it, and this leads to the brain cutting off all recognition of those parts that seem useless. This is particularly so if the limbs feel numb or the person is unaware of the position in which they are lying.

It is necessary to explain what has happened, and how important it is to acknowledge the disability. The limbs belong to the victim and no amount of help from anyone else can make them move and recover their strength and usefulness. It is common for people who are in hospital to think that someone else is going to get them better. The doctors, and particularly the physiotherapist can encourage, guide and instruct, but they cannot get inside and pull the strings. Sometimes the damage caused is too great to overcome, but recovery to a greater or lesser degree is possible in almost all cases.

I once treated a man who had a massive stroke and one side of his body was quite useless. He would make no attempt to perform the movements I asked him to do because he thought he would never get better. I asked him if he wanted to be a vegetable for the rest of his life, and he said that if he could not go back to work he might as well be. Eventually I persuaded him that even if he could not work he could at least get about at home; feed himself, and go to the lavatory when he wanted to. This he understood. From that day he worked harder at getting better than anyone I have known. Not only could he walk about, but he went back to work. I have told this story to illustrate the importance of the willingness to get better, though I do not mean to give the impression that if someone works hard enough he will *always* get better; some strokes cause too much damage to permit such a recovery, but with the use of aids a fairly normal life can be lived at home among the family.

To the layman, one of the unexpected results is lack of emotional control, which is especially distressing for men who find themselves crying because they have achieved something new, or are glad to see a visitor. Sometimes emotional responses are reversed, laughing when upset and crying when happy. Loss of memory, or areas of memory, and the inability to make the smallest decisions are common.

Changes in personality may occur; irritability and selfishness are the most common, though love and affection felt for family and friends is usually unaltered. Lack of concentration and the inability to realise the seriousness of their situation are very common in people who are paralysed on the left side.

Speech defects   The speech disturbances caused by a stroke are of three types, each of which may be of varying severity. The greatest disability is called *aphasia*. This means the total loss of the ability to form words and to understand anything said or written. Even the simplest commands or questions are met with a blank stare of total incomprehension. Enormous patience and understanding are required by those who are around a person in this position. Imagine the frustration caused by wondering what has happened, not only has all movement of one side of the body gone but he is unable to ask what has happened, or to understand any attempt at explanation. As recovery progresses understanding will return and gradually words be formed. The comprehension of commands and the names of objects will probably be achieved in a few days, but speech will take longer and may never fully recover. It is important to treat people in this position normally, because they are normal. There is nothing more irritating than being shouted at in slow monosyllables; they feel foolish enough anyway without this extra indignity.

Many people can say one or two phrases, or 'yes' and 'no', and that is all, and these are repeated every time they try to form a sentence or answer a question. It is rather like being tone deaf and singing lustily on the wrong note, but being convinced it is the right one. The words and language most closely related to normal life are usually those which are learned first.

Disturbance, rather than loss, of speech is called *dysphasia* or *dysarthria*. *Dysphasia* is divided into two groups. The inability to express thoughts and name objects that are recognised, there being no loss of comprehension; and the ability to give names to objects and form sentences, but the inability to understand what is said by somebody else. *Dysarthria* is usually a milder form of defect, when understanding and expression are both present but many words are pronounced wrongly: words are used that mean something to the speaker but to nobody else. The degree to which mistakes are made varies widely from the odd word to being hardly intelligible. An extremely helpful book for stroke sufferers with speech and communication problems is *A Stroke in the Family* by Valerie Eaton Griffith, published by Penguin.

Speech can be stimulated by those around encouraging the person to talk. By asking the names of familiar objects and getting them to repeat words after you, they relearn forgotten vocabulary. It may be necessary to break the word up in syllables and master each one separately before trying the whole word. Reassurance that they do not appear ridiculous when making mistakes helps them to try harder; many people will not even try for fear of failure or ridicule, so it is best not to press it when there are other people about. A sense of humour about the situation relaxes tension and enables them to form words more accurately, and indeed they sometimes say something quite spontaneously when not really trying. There is no need to be embarrassed if it is difficult to understand. Ask them to try again and suggest to them words they might be trying to say. If false teeth are worn make sure they are properly fitted. Nobody can speak clearly without teeth, or with ill-fitting dentures that keep dropping out.

Many people are helped by a bunch of tags on a tape with everyday words on such as 'drink', 'glasses', etc., in fact anything they may need, but include 'sleep', and 'go away, please', so they can have some privacy and quietness when they want it. If they are in hospital a speech therapist may work with them, and if relatives can ask her advice on how to approach the situation at home it is a great help.

Disturbances of sensation and circulation

These symptoms are common and cause quite a lot of trouble. If the circulation becomes abnormal due to the nerves to the blood vessels being affected the limbs may become swollen and heavy, which makes them feel even more useless than they really are. It does lead to stiffness of joints and stagnation of fluid in the hand and foot, and if this occurs the blood must be returned up the limb by outside mechanical means. Putting the arm or leg up on a pillow for half-hour periods helps to drain the fluid down. Massage from the fingers and toes upwards is also effective when done in this position. If the whole leg is swollen an elastic stocking or bandage can be a help but both must be applied correctly (see chapter 8).

Alteration of sensation is extremely unpleasant and there is little that can be done about it. The limbs may be quite numb with the person having no idea where they are unless he actually looks for them. The main problem in these cases is the difficulty of moving even a normal limb if it cannot be felt. It also falls about, the arm dropping off the lap and straining the shoulder joint, or the foot getting caught round the leg of the chair or table and wrenching the knee. Care must be taken not to injure any of the joints in this way, and they should be placed in a normal position, and not allowed to fall about. Apart from the injuries sustained in this way it makes him look more abnormal than he is.

Numbness presents other problems of burns and cuts. A hot water bottle must not be too hot and should always have a cover on it; it is so easy for the paralysed leg to rest against it and be badly burned. This applies even when sensation is normal because although pain may be felt from the burn the leg may be too weak to be moved away from it. Care must be taken with the fitting of suitable shoes as well, particularly if there are hammer toes or bunions present. A sore on the toes takes many months to clear up; a wide fitting for women which has been proved very satisfactory is called 'Diana Broadway' and is available at most good shoe shops.

Exaggerated sensation also needs care in a different way. In this case it is the actual person who must be thought of, not the limbs, because altered sensation of this type causes highly exaggerated reaction to heat, cold, and pain. Movements may be difficult to perform as every joint is excruciatingly painful. It is no good saying 'I can't be hurting you', because as far as he is concerned it feels as if the arm is being twisted off. It is an exceptionally unpleasant and sick-making type of pain and although the movements are very important the pain must be taken into account. Take care when handling the limbs not to put too much pressure on the skin or dig the finger tips into the muscles.

Movement and rehabilitation

Rehabilitation can begin as soon as the initial shock has worn off. The joints on the affected side must be put through their full range of movement; the full range being the greatest distance the joint will move in each direction within its normal limits. To appreciate the normal limits, either try the movement on the good side or on somebody else who is normal. Carry the movements out at least twice a day, preferably on a bed, but the arm can be done sitting in a chair. The friend or relative who performs the movements should go through them slowly and deliberately giving the muscles a chance to use what power they have. Pain may interfere due to hypersensitivity of the skin and joints but should be put up with if possible. If the pain is allowed to limit movement too drastically the joints become stiff and even more painful.

It is vital to maintain the normal patterns of movement; if the limb is held still for any length of time the brain dismisses it, and the impulse pathways along which the messages are sent become blocked. Then, there are not only weak muscles to contend with but re-education of the nerve pathways as well. A sign that this might be happening is when the person will not look towards the affected side and when asked to move it automatically does the movement with the good side, as if the other does not exist. This is particularly common among people with a weak left side.

After the movements described below have been carried out try them all again but with the person doing them himself as far as possible. Do not help until it is evident that it cannot be done unaided; very often he will say he cannot do it before he has even tried. Although repetition and constant effort on his part are vital, it is unwise to continue for too long at one time because despondency soon sets in if the movements are not forthcoming. Regaining movement is a long, slow and tedious job but without sustained effort over a period of time it will never be regained.

It is sometimes helpful to try moving both sides together, or is facilitated by asking him to close his eyes while performing the movement with the good side, at the same time remembering what the actual movement feels like. Then, while still aware of the feel of the movement he should try to repeat it with the other side.

When moving the affected side always make him look at it and be conscious of it, though this can be difficult, as many people lose a great deal of the power of concentration; but concentration like the muscles can be re-educated.

Movements for the arm and leg

Perform the movements in a half-lying position on a bed with the weak arm supported on a pillow.

Shoulder

1 Lift the arm straight up over the head.
2 With the elbow bent and the forearm lifted so it is level with the shoulder, rotate the arm towards the floor, and then upwards towards the ceiling.
3 Put the hand behind the head, and then behind the small of the back.

Elbow

1 Bend the hand up to the mouth then straighten the elbow turning the palm towards the floor.

Wrist

1 Hold the forearm just above the wrist with one hand and move the hand forward and back with the other.
2 Rotate the hand towards the floor and then towards the ceiling.

Hand

1 Straighten the fingers right out, first altogether, then each one individually.
2 Close the fingers up into a fist.
3 Move the thumb away from the palm then across towards the little finger. This is a very important movement which is vital for gripping effectively.

Hip

1 Bend the knee onto the chest; supporting the leg under the knee and the foot, straighten out. Take care to control the leg if it is floppy to avoid damage to the knee joint.
2 With the leg straight, roll the leg in so the toes touch the other foot, and then roll it away.
3 To effect a backward movement of the hip bend the opposite leg up onto the chest.

Knee

1 Bend the knee by sliding the heel along the bed to touch the seat.
2 Straighten it out again.

Ankle   1 With the knee straight push the foot up past the right angle, then down to point the toes to the ground. The upward movement is very important when walking to enable the foot to clear the ground.

Foot   1 Hold firmly across the top of the foot and twist the sole to face the other foot, then twist outwards (see also chapter 14).

There is one puzzling phenomenon about the movements of the limbs which is called *apraxia*. In a person whose weakness is fairly slight the ability to move is present, but when asked to move he seems incapable of doing so, though he may have just made the same movement without thinking about it. It is necessary to understand that there is some block in the passing of messages provoking voluntary movement; that is, the harder he tries the less likelihood there is of any movement being performed, but five minutes later he may reach out to drink a cup of tea. It is very irritating unless it is understood, and many people with the best will in the world are thought lazy and uncooperative; they also seem unable to explain what is happening.

Spasticity   After a period of time varying from weeks to months the weak muscles may lose their flaccidity and become spastic. The inhibiting control from the brain on the spinal cord is decreased, so it becomes hyper-excitable and sends off impulses for the muscles to contract continuously. Only certain muscle groups are affected and create a typical posture and particular disabilities.

In the upper limb the major groups affected are those which bend the arm and hand and those which draw it close to the side of the body, or adduct it. In the lower limb the extensors or straighteners and the adductors, which pull the leg in towards the other, are affected. So, in more detail, the arm is held tightly against the side, the elbow is bent and the forearm lies across the front of the body, the wrist is flexed and the fingers curled into the palm. The leg is held straight at the knee, the hip is slightly bent, and when the weight is taken off it the whole leg swings across in front of the other; the foot is pointed down towards the ground, and turned in so the weight is taken on the outer border. This pattern adopted by the leg is one of the major causes of loss of balance and the inability to walk.

Spasm patterns in the arm and leg

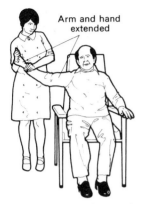

Pulling out a spastic arm

If the spasm is not counteracted it becomes stronger and stronger making the limbs useless, rigid and painful; the shoulder, wrist and hand being the worst affected. To a certain extent the spasm can be tired out and so the aim of all movements at this stage is to this end. The limb must be pulled out in the opposite direction to that in which the spasm is pulling. The elbow is pulled away from the side and the whole arm straightened at a right angle to the shoulder. The wrist is pulled back and the fingers straightened.

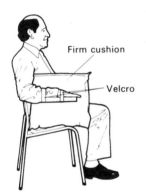

Velcro holding a spastic arm in position

If the spasm is very strong it can be a struggle to get the arm in this position, but if held there for a few minutes with a slight stretch on the whole arm it will slowly relax. It is also a help, sometimes, to hold onto the fingers and shake out the whole arm, exerting traction at the same time. Active movement by the person concerned also helps to counteract the spasm.

Having reduced the spasm the arm must not be allowed to spring back into its accustomed position. While sitting in a chair put a firm cushion between the arm and the side and lay the forearm along the arm of the chair; it may be necessary to hold it in position by a couple of straps round the forearm and wrist and attach it to the chair. Velcro sewn or stuck onto the chair arm is a convenient method.

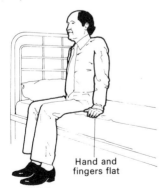

Leaning the weight through the weak arm

Many people advocate holding a ball or a tightly rolled bandage in the hand to prevent the fingers curling too much. I do not agree with this method. The spasm is caused by over excitability and the object in the hand is a constant source of stimulation and encourages the fingers to curl over even further. It is similar to putting something in a baby's palm; the fist immediately closes round it. The bearing of weight through a limb is a very effective way of controlling spasm and one reason why the leg usually recovers more fully than the arm, but weight can be taken through the arm by sitting on the edge of a firm bed or couch and placing the hand flat on the bed beside the seat. It may be necessary for someone else to hold the elbow straight while the body weight is leaned over the arm.

Using the weak leg as a prop

Weight evenly distributed
on both feet

Weight distribution

The main movements for the leg are to pull it out away from the other, and to bend the knee up onto the chest, at the same time pulling the foot up. The difficult thing is to keep the foot up while the knee is straightened which is an essential pattern in walking. In people with strong spasm a leg iron fitted into the shoe is used to control it. As with the arm, the spasm in the leg is greatly helped by bearing weight, so exercise standing up and holding onto a firm chair with the feet fairly wide apart and the legs straight helps to strengthen muscles and reduce spasm. Care must be taken to make sure the weight is evenly distributed on both feet because a lot of people keep all their weight on the good leg and only use the weak one as a prop.

Rehabilitation

Exercises for the arm and leg and for stretching out the spasm must be done at least twice a day and become a routine part of life; it is not a thing that can be allowed to lapse after a time.

Straightening the fingers

Lifting the arm

Reducing spasm in the arm
and hand

The person must be taught to lift the weak arm over the head by grasping the wrist with the other hand. He can also usefully spend time straightening the fingers.

The arm and leg are very obviously weak, but a stroke involves the whole of one side of the body which includes the muscles of the stomach, back and side as well as the facial muscles.

The face   Weak facial muscles are common and cause some distress. The face looks very obviously lopsided with the corners of the eye and the mouth drooping down and the cheek and neck sagging; they must be made to work again just like the other muscles that are affected. The use of a mirror is helpful and efforts should be made to close the eyes tightly and open them very wide. The nostrils can be flared out and the cheeks sucked in and puffed out. The mouth can be pursed as in whistling and the lips pulled into a wide grin.

Getting out of bed   Whenever helping a stroke sufferer *always stand on the weak side*. It would seem more natural to hold the strong arm but if you do this the person cannot even support his or her body with the good arm. The good leg is taking the weight, the good arm is being clutched by someone else, which then leaves the paralysed side quite unsupported, making the poor victim completely helpless and panic-stricken. The tendency is to fall towards the paralysed side and if no support is forthcoming he will crash down without even being able to put out a hand to break the fall. If he is tall it is impossible to prevent him falling from the good side; the helper can also be pulled over by the top-heavy weight she is trying to save.

The helper must never help more than absolutely necessary; it is only by the person using his own powers to the utmost that any recovery will be possible, and only after he has tried very hard should any assistance be given.

Encouragement and praise at each success helps to overcome the feeling of despair and uselessness which is so common, and confidence in the helper is vital to enable steps to be taken and progress made.

The first time out of bed is a big test and will show how great the disability is. Most people are very unsteady and often feel giddy after some days in bed and the circulatory disturbance in the brain, so everything should be done slowly, taking plenty of time. First of all the person should pull his or her

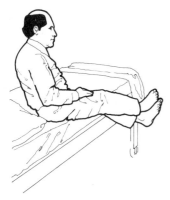

Using the strong leg to assist the weak one

body into the upright position by using the stomach muscles. (The helper may need to give a little support by placing one hand under the weak arm.) Then the sufferer should lift his or her legs to the edge of the bed; if the weak leg cannot move itself slip the good one underneath it and with the ankles crossed both legs can be moved together.

The helper prevents the weak foot sliding on the floor

Slide the legs off the bed and sit squarely on the edge, with the hands supporting the body on each side. Always try to make the weak side perform the same movements as the good one. Sit for a few minutes on the edge of the bed and try to maintain the balance of the body in that position. It will take a little while to get used to the idea of the balance being lopsided.

Borrow a walking aid from the Red Cross, but if one is not available place the back of a firm chair in front for the person to hold on to. Put the chair that is going to be sat in at a right angle to the bed and a couple of feet away from it. It is wise to use two helpers the first time until the degree of disability has been assessed. It also gives confidence to all concerned. With a helper supporting under the weak arm, not clutching it, ask the person to slide off the edge of the bed and stand on the floor holding on to the back of the chair. Most people find it comforting to have something to hold on to. The weak foot may slide on the floor and it can be kept in place by the helper's foot being used as a stop.

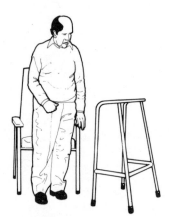

Putting the good hand on the chair before sitting down

The next step is to turn round ready to sit in the chair (see p. 95). The helper will probably have to push the weak leg into position, with the legs against the front of the chair, and the *good hand must be put down on to the arm of the chair before sitting down.*

Sitting down

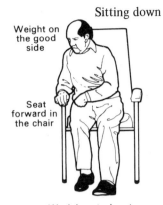

Weight on the good side

Seat forward in the chair

Weak leg stuck out

Sitting incorrectly

A person who has had a stroke often throws himself down in a chair, the good shoulder hitting the back of it first, and he remains sitting with all his weight on one side and his seat forward in the chair.

Turning towards the weak side when sitting down

To counteract this, ask him to sit down slowly and to bend forward as he goes down so that his seat touches the chair first and is right in the back of it. At the same time ask him to turn towards the weak side and this will enable him to land squarely on both buttocks.

Having sat in the chair with the seat well back and the weight square, the weak foot must be placed at a right angle to the knee and not allowed to stretch out and swing across towards the other leg. The arm can be supported on a pillow to prevent it being held tightly against the body or can be held on the arm of the chair as I have described for a spastic arm on p. 31.

The trunk

Trunk muscles are as important for sitting, standing, and walking as the legs, and weakness down one side makes balance difficult. When sitting unsupported the body either falls

Crab-like gait

towards the weak side, or backwards, and tends to slump to one side when spending any length of time in a chair. As well as re-educating the weak muscle groups, those on the other side of the body can be made to work harder and help in supporting the trunk. The shoulder tends to be pulled down by the weight of the arm and when walking either hangs down loosely in front of the body, or with a combination of weak side muscles leaves the whole side behind and a rather crab-like gait is adopted.

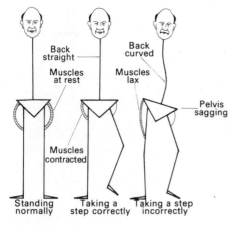

Diagram to show weak hip muscles allowing the pelvis to sag and the back to bend

Two of the most important muscle groups in walking are those that form the side of the waist and the hip, and enable the leg to be lifted and swung through to form a step. The waist muscles of one side work with the hip muscles of the other to hold the pelvis level while the step is taken. If the waist muscles are weak the leg cannot be lifted to clear the ground as the foot swings through, and if the hip muscles are weak the pelvis collapses towards the leg that is trying to take the step.

Clearly this is a great handicap and must be corrected if at all possible. The following movements will help to strengthen the trunk muscles.

1 Sitting squarely on a hard chair with the thighs well supported; lift the weak shoulder upwards and backwards as if bracing the shoulders.

2 Sitting as above, twist the body from the waist to look over one shoulder, then twist the other way to look over the other.

3 Sitting well back in a hard armchair with the elbows supported on the arms (the weak one may have to be held in place), lift one buttock up off the chair then the other. It is necessary to push down on the arms of the chair to get a purchase to lift from.

4 Sitting in a chair, lean against the back and pull the body forward with the stomach muscles, not by pulling with the hands.

Standing up

As always, the helper must *stand on the weak side*. Make sure the feet are well under the body; the weak foot often slides out straight. The person should be asked to slide his seat forward on the chair, and to lean his head forward over the knees (see p. 97). The head should be level with the knees to enable the body to be raised up. With the good hand on the arm of the chair, and the aid ready in front, the body is pushed up by the hand on the chair and by pushing on the legs. The helper can support under the arm if necessary and prevent the weak foot from sliding by placing her foot in front of it. As soon as the person is standing upright the feet should be placed slightly apart and the weight taken evenly on both legs, which will hold the weak one in position, and help to counteract any spasm that may be present. The heel should be down on the floor, but if the knee bends in the effort to get it there it must be supported by the helper's knee.

Helper using her knee to support the weak leg

A word about '*clutching*': many helpers are prone to hang on to their charges as a drowning man clutches a straw, and one wonders who is helping whom. Whatever the disability, the only contact should be the hand under the arm. The point of the helper is only to do the little bit that is necessary; too much help is just as useless as too little. The person must be allowed to use his own balance, and his own muscles; if the helper is trying to balance him too it upsets the state of equilibrium (see chapter 13, section on 'Helping the elderly to walk').

Walking
Theoretically, stroke sufferers are taught to walk with a tripod walking stick, but from experience I have found that old people regain their confidence and normal gait more easily by using a walking frame. The good hand can hold one side, and the helper can either hold the other in place or slip it through a strap attached to the hand piece. Having the frame in front reduces the fear of falling, and having to put both hands forward is very beneficial in two respects. A stroke sufferer often develops a crab-like walk and the arm either hangs down in front of the body or is held in spasm at the shoulder and wrist. Use of the frame prevents both; if the hands are level, the body must be level, and having to stretch them out on to the frame counteracts the spasm.

The use of a walking frame (right) corrects the crab-like gait and stretches the arm

The use of a bandage in walking a stroke sufferer

Before beginning to walk check that the person is standing as straight as possible, and that the legs are apart with the weak one taking some weight. Firm support under the arm will give confidence and ensure that the helper is ready to take some of the weight if necessary. Many people can stand quite well with all the weight on the good leg and the weak one just acting as a prop. Check too that the weak foot is flat on the ground, if it is very floppy or in spasm it may be rolled onto its outside border and will cause damage to the ankle joint if a step is taken on it. It is important to remember that in many cases the person will have no idea whether his foot is flat or not. If the leg is very weak a bandage can be looped round the foot and the ends held in the helper's hand to help pull the leg through to take a step.

When all is ready, the frame is moved forward slightly and the weak leg put forward to take a step, at the same time preventing it from swinging across the other one by pressure on the bandage. When it is firmly on the ground the good leg makes a step, the weak one being supported by the helper's knee, if necessary, as the weight is taken on it. It is common for people to fall slightly backwards as the good leg comes through; to counteract this he must be told to push off with the toes of that foot and as the leg swings through to bring the top half of the body as well so that the weight is taken on the weak leg. It is the weight being left behind that causes the backward lean.

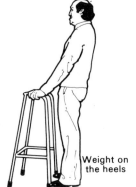

Weight is *through* the leg

Push off with this foot

Weight on the heels

To show the weight being brought through when taking a step

The weak leg is kept well out to allow the weight to fall between the feet

The helper can assist by an upward and forward pressure under the arm. It is easy to feel how much help should be given; if there is gross weakness a great deal of support is required and at the knee also, but with less severe disabilities he will move the leg himself and be fairly good at holding himself upright.

As I have said, a person who has had a stroke falls towards the weak side and may lean quite heavily on the helper. The best way to counteract this is to ask him to try and lean well over towards the good side, and at the same time to keep the weak leg well out to the side by the use of the bandage if he cannot do it himself. The weight of the body should fall between the legs.

If the balance of both is correct a large person can be supported by a fairly small helper.

Gradually, less support can be given until he is walking unaided. How long it takes will vary from person to person, but it will not be a few days, more likely a few weeks or months, but however long he should not be bullied and made to feel he is not progressing fast enough: it is a guaranteed way of making him give up altogether.

The instructions I have given may sound complicated and pedantic but they are all necessary for re-education of walking and balance. The position of the leg and the amount of help given, the control of the body weight, and the use of the bandage make all the difference between walking well and falling over. The details are important, a stroke victim cannot walk when just being propped up.

Dressing To enable rehabilitation and confidence to progress it is important that the elderly person should feel as normal as possible. A time comes when the attitude of 'patient' must be discarded even if there is a good deal of residual disability. The person should get up each day at a normal time and dress him- or herself as far as possible. Dressing is as much a part of getting better as walking is, and he or she should be encouraged to do it personally. A man can simply wear a shirt and trousers, shoes and socks; and a woman a blouse and cardigan, and a skirt or button-through dress that is easy to put on. As long as sitting up unaided is possible the majority of people should be able to put most things on for themselves. They should dress sitting in an armchair or sitting on the edge of the bed, with the walking frame in front of them, and use as many short cuts as possible. Whenever putting on shirts and cardigans or coats always put the weak arm in first and then pull the sleeve right up to the armpit; the rest of the garment can be thrown round the shoulders and the sleeve retrieved by the good arm. Follow Tables 1 or 2, and as in all aspects of rehabilitation, no help should be given unless it is really necessary. See also chapter 16.

Normal living From the first time of getting out of bed *the image of the disabled invalid must be abandoned.* The 'stroke patient' becomes a normal person who just happens not to be able to do some things. Two stages follow: The first six months to a year are concerned with rehabilitation; the active process of re-educating and strengthening muscles; mastering the everyday tasks of dressing, eating and washing, and the necessary movements of walking, sitting, getting in and out of bed and

Table 1
Dressing for Men

Clothing	Alterations	Method
Vest		Put the weak arm in first
Shirt	Elastic cuff-links	Put the weak arm in first
Pants }* Trousers}	Clip the two together with clothes pegs. Use stretch braces	Clip pants inside the trousers. Keep hold of the braces. Throw the two articles on to the floor. Put the feet in and pull up above the knees. Slip the braces over the shoulders and either lift one side of the seat up after the other to pull the trousers up, or stand up
Socks*		Cross one foot over the opposite knee
Shoes	Elastic laces	Slip on, if necessary use long-handled shoe horn
Tie	Replace the back with elastic	Slip over the head
Jacket		As for shirt

* If it is easier, socks, trousers and pants can be put on before putting the legs over the edge of the bed. This saves bending down if balance is not good.

Table 2
Dressing for Women

Clothing	Alterations	Method
Bra	Make opening down the front and fasten with velcro	Put on like a coat
Blouse } Cardigan}	Poppers or velcro instead of buttons	Put on like a coat Put on like a coat
Pants	Use elastic pants instead of a corset. Sew buttons on the front and back for suspenders	As for men's trousers, only use elastic instead of braces
Stockings	Sew large loops on suspenders and attach to stockings	Use a stocking gutter
Skirt	Undo side seam and use as a wrap-over skirt, fasten with velcro	Wrap round or put over head
Shoes	Wear casuals or use elastic laces	Slip on, use long-handled shoe horn

using the toilet. Officially the time for maximum recovery is two years, but in my experience most recovery is gained in the first nine to twelve months if proper treatment has been carried out during that period. There may still be a good deal of weakness and spasm, particularly in the arm, and tasks that others do automatically are laboriously difficult. Of course, the degree of recovery is entirely individual but the amount of effort and will involved has tremendous bearing on the end result.

When the point is reached when no further recovery is possible, the time has come to readapt the pattern of life within the limits of the disability. I do not mean by becoming resigned to being an invalid, but by living as fully as possible. Many women who have had strokes return to running their homes; not as fully as before but well enough to give satisfaction and a sense of achievement. Often when people return home from hospital or are able to take a fuller role in the household the relatives start treating them like invalids again by not allowing them to do anything. Not only is the stroke imposed upon them, but a feeling of uselessness and boredom as well (see chapter 1).

All the advice and help previously described for the guidance of relatives looking after a stroke victim must *be transferred to him*; he must gradually take on the responsibility of caring for himself. If a home is adequately fitted with gadgets most people who have had a stroke should be able to manage.

The daily chores of washing up, laying the table, dusting, and peeling the vegetables can all be done with one hand if necessary, and a man should be encouraged to do these and other light jobs around the house even if he does take a long time over them. It only takes one hand to drink a pint of beer, if the pub is near enough or transport available, and country people do not need two hands to lean on a pen and keep up with the prices at the market. Most people can go and sit on a bench and watch the world go by, so it is not inevitable that someone who has had a stroke must be housebound and spend the greater part of the day indoors in a chair (see chapter 16).

4 Fractures

Fractured 'hip' Fracture of the 'hip' is a very common accident in the elderly, but is not as serious today as it used to be. Although described loosely as the 'hip', the fracture is at the upper end of the thigh bone, and may or may not involve the hip joint.

First aid Indications that a fracture has been sustained are shock, and pain in the upper part of the thigh with the leg rolled outwards and the outer border of the foot lying along the ground. The patient is pale, clammy and cold and the breathing may be rapid and shallow. The immediate need is to reduce the effect of shock. The injured person should not be moved but laid flat on the floor with a pillow under the head, and covered with a blanket. Many old people suffer from heart disease and may be unable to lie quite flat without becoming breathless and their lips turning blue, in which case they should be propped up enough to allow normal breathing. The blanket used for covering is only to prevent chilling, a person in a shocked condition should not be overheated; the coldness and the paling of the skin is due to the blood being used in the vital organs, and if too much warmth is added it returns to the skin leaving the heart and injury site depleted. Drinks of hot tea or alcohol should not be given; if any fluid is taken it should be sips of cool water only. If shock appears to be severe the uninjured leg can be raised on a pillow to aid the return of blood to the heart. Having made sure the patient is as comfortable as possible phone for an ambulance.

An old person on his own may be able to reach a pillow and a blanket if he has fallen by the bed, which is common, but if not, anything within reach can be used to prevent chilling; even a small floor rug or a newspaper is better than nothing.

Treatment In all cases where it is possible the person undergoes an operation during which the bone-ends are returned to their correct position and held in place by a metal plate.

Sometimes, if severe arthritis is present and the fracture is near the joint, a new head of femur is inserted; that is, the ball part of the ball and socket joint.

The site of the fracture is made quite rigid and as soon as the shock of the operation has worn off, usually in about forty-eight hours, the old person is helped up to sit in a chair. As soon as possible, probably the following day, the physiotherapist will help him to walk again. In theory crutches are used to take the weight off the injured leg for several weeks, but the majority of old people who have been thoroughly shaken by the fall and the operation are in no state to go hopping unsteadily about on crutches. Their balance is made worse than usual by pain and stiffness, and they are very frightened of falling over again. In my experience better results are produced in a kinder way by using a walking frame. If most of the weight can be taken on the arms so much the better, but using the leg a little does not seem to cause undue pain or cause further damage, but it does enable a normal walking pattern to be re-established quickly and so avoid long weeks of re-educating a normal gait. It seems strange, but a short period of time, plus discomfort and stiffness, either make people forget how to walk, or make them too apprehensive even to try.

A fractured 'hip' is a serious injury and causes extensive damage to surrounding structures. Immediately after the operation the leg will be very sore and stiff, but like a cut finger if it is moved straight away the elasticity of the skin and muscles returns quickly. If allowed to lie rigid and immobile for days it becomes very painful and the muscles go into spasm to protect it, and regaining movement is an uphill task.

Acute confusion is an occasional complication, partly due to the pain and partly due to the change of environment. The only treatment necessary is reassurance and understanding until the old person has become reorientated and aware of the situation.

Physiotherapy   In hospital a physiotherapist will come every day right from the beginning. On the first day she will teach breathing exercises and foot movements to prevent a chest infection and thrombosis in the leg, because, although the elderly person will be getting up very soon, the effect of the anaesthetic can precipitate complications. She will also teach contractions of the quadriceps muscles: those down the front of the thigh which are of prime importance in regaining the use of the leg. Without these muscles the knee cannot bear the weight of the body, and due to the injury they will have become very weak. The physiotherapist can usually only see people once a day, and therefore asks them to carry out the exercises on their own at intervals. Most old people forget to do them, so relatives can help by reminding them during visiting hours.

Regaining movement in the hip joint is, of course, very important, and will be facilitated by putting the leg in two slings to support it, allowing a free swinging movement; first lying on the back and then on the side. Re-education of walking will be continued every day with the help of equipment and parallel bars in the physiotherapy department.

Full movement rarely returns after an injury causing extensive damage, particularly in the elderly, and one of the main difficulties which arises is getting up from a chair. Aids for adapting the chair and gadgets for use when dressing are shown in chapter 16.

Very often the fractured leg becomes shorter than the other, but this is easily rectified by putting a raise on the shoe. This is a small thing but an important one, because walking with one leg shorter than the other not only causes arthritis in the good leg but in the back too. The weight is unevenly distributed on the joints and so wears the surfaces down in some places by undue pressure, and less than normal in others (see 'Osteo-arthritis' in chapter 2). The assessment of the correct amount of raise is best left to a physiotherapist or a surgical fitter because too much height creates the same problems as too little. If it has to be done at home varying thicknesses of wood should be placed under the foot of the short leg until the bony parts of the front of the hips are level. It is unlikely that the raise will need to be more than a half, or certainly three-quarters of an inch.

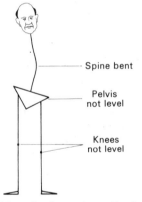

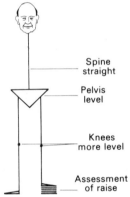

Measuring for a raise on the shoe

The results of this operation are usually very good providing the joint was fairly free from arthritis, and providing the person co-operates, though having the head of the femur replaced improves severe arthritis. Many old people get depressed after such a serious accident and think it will be the end for them, or think it is not worth all the effort required to get better, so much encouragement is necessary to stimulate the will to try hard. In some cases where the results are not as good as would be expected the matter should be looked into further. There may be some other reason, such as a small stroke which passed unnoticed in the excitement and quite likely caused the fall in the first place. It is also possible for the plate to slip or bend causing pain and making walking difficult.

Back to normal   As soon as the elderly person returns from hospital he must try to be as independent as possible, and the home adapted to his needs. Rails can be put up by steps and in the bathroom and lavatory; the bed can be brought downstairs and a chair can be raised or lowered to a suitable height.

As with all joint injuries and arthritis it is not good to sit around for long periods; standing still, too, creates pain and stiffness, so many short walks should be taken during the day, not necessarily outside, but just round the house to move the limbs and prevent muscles and joints from becoming 'set'.

One big problem is putting on shoes and socks. The hip will not bend sufficiently to put them on in the conventional manner, so another way must be used. Sit sideways on the edge of a chair and bend the knee as fully as possible so the heel is near the seat and the sock can be put on quite easily. Alternatively use a stocking gutter (see chapter 16).

All the exercises taught by the physiotherapist should be continued at least twice a day at home, and every possible precaution should be put into operation to prevent another fall (see chapter 16).

Fracture of the upper arm

This is another common fracture among the elderly, especially women, again sustained through a fall. The fracture is about level with the armpit and due to the nature of the fall the two pieces of bone are pushed into each other. There is shock, and extensive bruising over the shoulder area. Due to the bone ends being interlocked no outside support is necessary in the form of splints or plaster. If an old person has an arm immobilised by putting it in plaster she will probably never move it again because it becomes so stiff. Without any support the bone mends spontaneously and although full range of movement will not be recovered it will be usable and painless.

For the first twenty-four hours a sling can be worn to ease the initial pain and give time to get over the accident, but a large pad of cotton wool should be placed under the arm and in the bend of the elbow to absorb perspiration. After a few days attempts should be made to regain movement in the arm. This will be supervised by a physiotherapist at the hospital. The first thing will be to get the arm swinging, and when it is a little stronger it must be lifted up and put through all its movements. The sling should only be used for short periods if the arm aches badly, but as far as possible the arm should be used as normally as the pain allows.

One complication that can arise from this fracture is damage to the nerve which circles the bone at the level of the break. The first sign that this has happened will be tingling over the skin on the upper and outer part of the arm, just below the shoulder. General care must be taken of the hand and armpit, which become sore very quickly unless kept clean and dry.

Many people have great difficulty dressing, and as it will continue for several weeks it is worth altering some clothes to enable them to be put on without too much of a struggle. The straps of bras and petticoats can be undone and fastened with velcro, and the use of front opening dresses will save having to put them over the head.

After the accident the hospital will often admit an old person to one of the wards for a day or two, particularly if she lives alone; on discharge treatment is arranged in the physiotherapy department for which transport will be laid on. People living alone should ask for meals on wheels and a home help to tide them over until they can resume their own chores and cooking.

Fracture of the wrist   This fracture is also particularly common in women, and is sustained by putting out a hand to save a fall. The wrist is displaced and has to be 'set' under anaesthetic, after which plaster of paris is applied and worn from four to six weeks. After the plaster is applied there may be further swelling, so attention must be paid to the appearance of the fingers. They will already be swollen and bruised but if they increase in size still further and look bloated and blue the hospital should be contacted straight away; it is a sign that the plaster has become too tight and is interfering with the circulation of the hand.

During the time the plaster is on, the fingers should be exercised vigorously to increase the circulation and strengthen the muscles round the wrist. The arm should be raised above the head daily to make sure no arthritis is set up in the shoulder by the jolt received during the fall. The same applies to the elbow, it must be straightened right out and bent up fully.

The hand should be used as normally as the plaster allows; there are many jobs that can be done such as dusting, peeling potatoes, and general cleaning. After the plaster is taken off the wrist will be stiff and the grip very weak. Exercises and wax baths will be given at the hospital but all the exercises should be done several times a day at home too. Washing up is excellent therapy and the warm water makes movement easier, and wringing light articles of clothing is also very beneficial.

All activities should return to normal as soon as possible; the only exception being not to lift heavy things for a few weeks, particularly heavy saucepans full of water.

5 Parkinson's Disease

Symptoms

Mask–like face

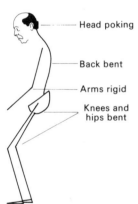

Head poking

Back bent

Arms rigid

Knees and hips bent

Parkinson's Disease: general picture

Parkinson's is a disease of very slow onset characterized by slowness and rigidity of movement. It is caused by malfunction of a specialised part of the brain concerned with voluntary movement, and is more common in men than women. The onset usually occurs between fifty and sixty-five, and is so slow that friends and relatives are not aware of the small alterations in bearing and reactions.

The muscles in the arms become rigid and cause a 'cog wheel' type of movement, which is slow and lacks purpose. The hands take on a characteristic position and develop a tremor called 'pill rolling'. The walk becomes a shuffle and often breaks into a run; the person has little control over movement and cannot start walking, or once going, has trouble in stopping. The rigidity of the muscles causes fatigue and pain, and the face takes on a typical expressionless, mask-like quality. If the muscles of the throat are involved the speech is slow and slurred. Those whose face and mouth are affected seem to be unaware of what is going on around them and laugh at a joke long after everyone else has forgotten about it. The voluntary movements involved in smiling, and indeed in all initiated actions, take so long to get into operation that their reactions seem very slow. In fact, until the disease is very advanced, the mental faculties are quite unaffected and the person sees, feels and experiences all that is going on. It is, of course, very embarrassing for him and should be treated as a normal reaction.

The general picture of a person with Parkinson's Disease shows the back bent with the chin poking forward, the arms held rigidly by the sides, and the hands stiff but performing the constant 'pill rolling' movements. The hips and knees are bent which tends to throw the weight forward making him very unsteady.

Treatment

As Parkinson's Disease is progressive, all treatment is directed towards the relief of discomfort and the prolonging of activity. Most people who have had Parkinson's Disease diagnosed will have had courses of physiotherapy treatment to help increase movement and maintain independence, but a few visits a week is not enough, and the person concerned should work continuously at home to maintain any improvement that is gained, or, if that is not possible to prevent further stiffening and limitation of movement.

Relief of pain

Aching and pain in the muscles are due to rigidity and poor circulation, but a lot can be done at home to ease them. The person must learn to relax the rigid muscles, but this can only be done after the circulation has been improved. Many people always feel cold due to lack of movement and poor circulation, which causes even greater stiffness. It is difficult to warm the whole body, but the use of a top electric blanket which can be left on is a big help, though it must, of course, be perfectly maintained and quite safe. The back is usually bent so a number of pillows are required to support the body fully. Once a satisfactory position has been gained the process of relaxation can begin. A deep breath is taken, and as it is released the whole body should be allowed to sink into the bed. It should create a feeling of the limbs being very heavy, and consciousness of the pillows and mattress pushing up against the back and legs. The deep breathing can continue at a natural speed, but an effort should be made to move the ribs *out* as the breath is drawn *in*. Normally the breathing is very shallow and the ribs hardly move at all, which creates a condition of inelasticity which predisposes towards chest infection. If it is possible to get into the bath the warmth of the water is an excellent relaxant, and full use should be made of the opportunity.

Mobility and posture   Due to rigidity and weakness of the muscles, the joints gradually become deformed; it is a very slow process and can go undetected for some while, so constant effort must be made to maintain full activity.

I said earlier that several pillows will be needed to support the spine, but efforts must be made to reduce the number by spending some time lying slightly flatter to allow the flexor muscles of the front of the body to stretch out. They become tight and act as a bowstring keeping the body bent.

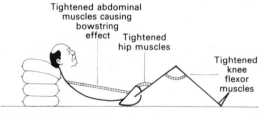

Bowstring effect of tightened abdominal muscles

This can be helped by pushing the head and shoulders back into the bed to make the muscles of the back stronger and to straighten the spine. While in the lying position all the joints should be moved through their full range: the arms raised over the head, the elbows stretched out, and the fingers straightened and bent up into a tight fist. The knees should be bent on to the chest and the feet pulled up and down from the ankles.

The rigidity of the muscles affects those of the trunk as well as the limbs and greatly hampers activity; the body is not flexible enough to correct imbalance and often results in falls. One way to improve this is to sit on a chair and try to twist round to look behind, the head should be turned first, followed by the shoulder; the movement must only take place at the waist, and should be repeated turning the other way. While sitting, circle the head round and round to release the rigidity in the neck muscles. Many people with Parkinson's Disease suffer badly with pain in the neck due to spasm and the poking forward position of the chin. Some time each day should be spent in front of the mirror trying to correct this. If a friend or relative can massage the back of the neck it relieves the tension considerably and reduces pain as well as increasing movement.

While in front of the mirror encourage facial muscles to be responsive. Try to smile, frown, blow the cheeks out, wink the eyes and whistle, and all as spontaneously as possible.

Tremor in the hands is an irritating and embarrassing symptom and is difficult to control, though it usually stops when activity of the hands begins, and can often be more easily controlled by holding something when at rest, such as a pipe or newspaper. The fine movements of the hands are difficult to perform and a great deal of practice is necessary to keep them useful. A piece of dough is a good aid and can be pinched, rolled, squeezed and modelled. Playing the piano is excellent exercise for the fingers, and typing also, which may become a useful skill if there is difficulty in writing normally.

Loss of semi-automatic movements such as swinging the arms and moving the legs while walking, combined with the

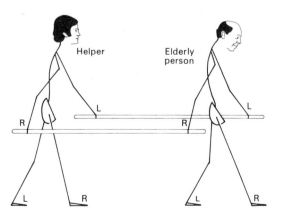

Walking in rhythm with two parallel sticks

characteristic inability to start a movement make walking very difficult indeed. Semi-automatic movements can be encouraged by the help of another person and two walking sticks. The helper stands behind holding the ends of the sticks, the elderly person holds the other ends; the arm-swinging movements can be started and kept moving rhythmically by the helper controlling the sticks.

When this is mastered the legs can be brought in by marking time, the helper calling out, 'left', 'right', 'left', 'right' while moving the sticks in co-ordination. Many people find it easier to do this to music with a one-two beat.

Stopping and starting exercises also need a helper. After the long delay before walking is commenced the steps become shorter and shorter, and faster and faster, until the body is moving along at a greater speed than the legs and can result in a fall, as there is inability to stop (see chapter 6). A helper walking with the person can keep one hand under the arm to propel him forward gently when starting, and restrain him slightly as he starts running; though he must also try and control himself. Commands of 'stop', 'start' and 'turn round' can be given quite frequently to give the opportunity to practise changes of direction and improve the balance at different speeds. Many falls are sustained when turning and due to the rigidity of the body it is usually the head that hits the ground first. All the time, while walking, efforts must be made to keep the back upright and the knees straight.

The amount of support necessary depends on how advanced the disease is, though most elderly sufferers feel safest with a walking aid. The type of aid depends on the degree of disability which will be assessed by the physiotherapist, but in my opinion the one with wheels in front is preferable. The ordinary type prevents running because it must be lifted up after each step, but it also prevents starting too, as there is a long pause before each step. The type with wheels enables a continuous walking pattern to be established, but the fact of there being something in front prevents running too. Those people who can start fairly easily and have more difficulty in stopping may find the one with wheels a little unnerving and may be better with the ordinary type.

Getting out of a chair is something that creates a problem for many people. Although when walking there is a tendency to lean forward, while sitting or just standing there is usually a 'backward tilt' (see chapter 6). To get up from the chair the basic principles apply of sitting on the edge of the chair, leaning well forward and pushing upwards and forwards while also pushing on the legs (see chapter 13). When sitting down the head must be bent well forward to put the seat right back in the chair to prevent falling backwards into it like a ramrod.

It is even more important with people who have Parkinson's Disease than with other old people not to make them hurry. Many relatives think they are being perverse by not getting up, or just bad tempered because they do not laugh; but the more sympathy, understanding and time they are given the better will be the results.

6 Falls and loss of balance

When an old person has a fall the question is often raised as to whether or not they should continue living in their own home. It is not only a matter of the person's health and the safety and accessibility of the house, but of the opinions and feelings of the person concerned. Many old people fear having to leave their home, and suffer much heart-ache; they would rather be there with the risks involved than in a home or hospital, whatever the conditions.

Causes of falls Often the real reason for a fall is never ascertained, or is masked by the injury sustained during the fall. A common example is the person who has a slight stroke, causing him to fall and fracture the 'hip'; by the time the hip is mended the symptoms of the stroke have gone.

High blood pressure causes giddiness, particularly when bending or after exertion. Low blood pressure does, too, but the giddiness is brought on by changes in position, such as suddenly standing up or getting out of bed. Many accidents happen at night when getting up to go to the lavatory; it is wise to sit on the edge of the bed for a minute before standing up.

Some falls are due to failing sight, though being aware of the problems and being particularly careful prevents many accidents. The danger is greatest at the time when the sight is only slightly impaired and the hazards are not fully realised. It is when the unexpected occurs, or something changes position that blind people fall. When visiting a person with bad sight always make sure the chair that was used is replaced exactly where it was. Urges to go round tidying things up should be curbed, because it hinders rather than helps.

Muscle weakness causing the knees to 'give way' is common, and is doubly dangerous because it may happen while crossing the road. This type of collapsing is most usual among people with arthritic knees and can be counteracted by doing exercises for the thigh muscles which support the knees (see chapter 14).

There are several diseases of the brain and nervous system, as well as the forms of arthritis responsible for weakness, loss of balance and deformity, which upset the mechanism of balance and posture. This is a complicated pattern created by the postural reflex in the brain, and the action of the muscles and joints. If any of these components becomes unbalanced the mechanism is disrupted, and falls occur.

Balance and posture Many falls, and inability or unwillingness to walk, are caused by loss of balance. Also, it is often the first indication that something may be wrong with some other function of the body. To be properly balanced the body should be straight with the weight passing through the ear, shoulder, hip, knee and just in front of the ankle. A deformity of one joint can be compensated for by a distortion at some other which corrects the balance and makes the weight still pass through the feet. If the weight is in front or behind the feet, or to either side of them as in a stroke patient, the body cannot maintain an upright position (figures a–d).

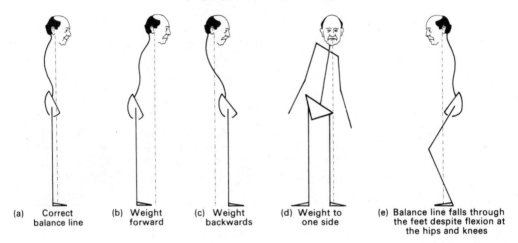

(a)   Correct balance line   (b) Weight forward   (c) Weight backwards   (d) Weight to one side   (e) Balance line falls through the feet despite flexion at the hips and knees

Deformity at the knees or hips can be caused by rheumatoid arthritis, osteo-arthritis, a long period in bed, or muscle weakness caused by some other disease, or lack of use. To remain upright when the knees are bent, the hips and ankles must bend also to compensate for them. Similarly, deformity at the hips, for the same reasons, and including fracture of the 'hip', requires compensatory bending at the knees and ankles. The weight still falls from the ear to the ankle in spite of compensatory shifts from the midline in between (figure e). People with such posture usually fall from some associated abnormality such as weak thigh muscles which 'give way', or sudden pain from the limb adopting an unaccustomed position.

It is fairly uncommon for the weight to fall in front of the 'balance line' except in people who have Parkinson's Disease. In these cases the balance is not disturbed until movement has begun; as their steps become shorter and faster the top half of the body gathers momentum while the legs are losing it. Parkinson's sufferers usually develop the bent hip and knee pattern described above due to weakness of the muscles. A walking aid is helpful (see chapter 5).

The weight falling behind the 'balance line', or 'backward tilt', is common, particularly among those who have spent some time in bed, or slumped back in a chair. One cause of posture of this type is disorientation of the centre in the brain responsible for control of balance. If a person has spent a long time leaning back in a chair or bed the centre begins to think that this is the normal position to be in. When the time comes to get up the body is leaning backwards from the straight line without being aware of it. The person concerned also feels as if he is straight, and if pushed into an upright position feels as if he will fall on his face and consequently resists. Fortunately this upset is fairly easy to rectify by ensuring that the body is upright or even leaning forward slightly when sitting in a chair or in bed, though it will take several weeks (see chapters 11 and 13).

People suffering from this disturbance are quite unable to stand without being supported, but even when they are being held the feet may slide out from under them. They should be on a non-slip surface and the helpers can place one of their feet in front of the old person's to prevent them sliding forward. Disturbance of the balance centre may also be due to a stroke or some other disease of the brain or nervous system.

Fear of falling, or being dropped, can create a 'backward tilt' position; the feeling of falling forward onto the floor is counteracted by pulling back in the opposite direction. People who are frightened enough to produce this reaction are usually rigid from head to foot and refuse to put one foot in front of the other. Great patience, and assurance that they will not fall, must be backed up by physical help, and making quite sure that they do not fall. Confidence in the helpers is everything. A walking frame provides something to hold on to. One with front wheels is best because it never has to be picked up off the floor to be moved (the action of picking it up encourages the 'backward tilt' position). The weight can be kept firmly leaning forward on it and helps stimulate momentum and makes walking more automatic and normal.

One other cause of 'backward tilt' is the comparatively simple one of painful feet (see chapter 8). If foot strain or a bunion causes pain in the ball of the foot the tendency is to take all the weight off it, which results in throwing the body weight backwards and taking it through the heels. If no other problems at all are present an otherwise fit person will compensate for this by bending forward at the hips.

Weight falling to the side of the 'balance line' is only present in people who have not regained their balance control after a stroke (see chapter 3).

How to get up or attract attention

Falls do occur despite care and safety precautions, and the problem arises of how to get up off the floor; or, if that is impossible, to attract attention. Even if the fall has caused no serious damage it creates a considerable state of shock in old people. They feel very frightened and shaken, and before attempting to get up should lie as flat as possible for a few minutes to recover.

Most people can move themselves along the floor to a chair, and with its support, get themselves into a side-sitting position; and from there into kneeling with the arms on the chair. After a breather they can bend one knee up (the strongest one) and push themselves up into the chair.

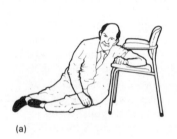

(a)

(b)

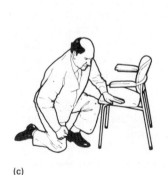

(c)

(d)

The right side is paralysed

Getting up off the floor

If another person is present and able to help he should avoid trying to lift the old person bodily off the floor. It is almost impossible, and easier for both parties if the previous instructions are carried out, with the helper giving a lift under the arm. The helper should stand on the weak side of someone who has had a stroke. If the old person is quite helpless it may be necessary to lift him or her, but this should only be done by two people and after they have made sure there is no injury. If in doubt, telephone the doctor. Before attempting to lift, put a chair as close as possible and put the person in a sitting position; put one hand under the arm and a foot in front of theirs to prevent it slipping as they are raised off the floor.

If the person is alone and it is impossible to get up, he or she should reach for a pillow or cushion, or roll up a rug to put under the head. Try, also, to prevent catching cold; if the fall occurs in the bedroom a blanket will be fairly handy, otherwise a thin carpet, or even a newspaper can be used. This is particularly important if it is night time because it may be several cold hours before help will come.

The method used to attract attention depends largely on where the house is situated. Social Service departments or voluntary groups in some towns or village centres fit a bell or light system which is relayed to the front gate to attract passers-by. If this service is not available a sports whistle can be worn on a string round the neck. It is loud and can be heard for some distance; or keep a placard permanently beside a front window. In emergencies the placard with 'Please Help' or some such message can be raised to the window while sitting on the floor.

The problem is much more serious in rural areas and advantage should be taken of the Social Service scheme to install telephones for old people who live alone. It must be low enough to reach from the floor, and a socket put upstairs in the bedroom as well as downstairs. It should be taken up each night, because it is no use if a fall occurs in the middle of the night and the telephone is downstairs. See also chapter 16, p. 148.

7 Bronchitis

Bronchitis is a common disease in Britain, and it can be helped quite a lot by correct day-to-day management. It is particularly prevalent in the industrial areas and is irritated by fog, cold and damp as well as cigarette smoking. It is caused initially by a germ, or continuous irritation from fumes and smoky atmospheres. The lining of the numerous tubes in the lungs becomes inflamed causing it to produce far more mucus than it would normally. Shortness of breath is a major symptom caused by the tubes being blocked by the mucus and preventing sufficient air from entering the lungs. They become congested and the sufferer tries to clear them by constant coughing, particularly at night when large amounts of mucus collect there. In most elderly bronchitics the condition is usually chronic; after several years of winter attacks the cough is present all the year round. Some sputum is brought up all the time, but particularly in the mornings, and is frothy and white. If it becomes thick and yellow, call the doctor, as it is a sign of an infection in the lungs.

Acute attacks can be treated, and in many cases avoided if caught in time. Special care should be taken with colds and flu, and at the first sign of the chest being affected treatment should be sought. As soon as mucus builds up in the tubes the irritation caused by its presence makes them produce even more, and as they become blocked the lungs struggle harder to draw in more air. The muscles between the ribs and those in the neck can be seen straining to make the chest move enough to allow air to enter. The chest and ribs become stiff and the lungs lose their natural elasticity and produce even greater quantities of mucus.

Being able to clear the tubes of mucus and keep the chest mobile makes life more comfortable and reduces the ultimate damage that can be done to the lungs. Many people try to clear the lungs by a continuous struggling cough; they go red in the face, feel giddy and do not stop to draw breath until they produce some sputum. It comes up eventually but leaves them exhausted, having put a tremendous strain on the heart and lungs. The most effective way to cough is to take a deep breath in, using the bottom of the lungs; that is, by pushing the stomach *out* as the air is drawn *in*. On breathing out again the mouth should be open and the air forced out through the back of the throat making a 'rushing wind' noise. If several breaths are taken like this, the sputum is brought up from the lungs and is fairly easy to expel with one or two strong coughs. If it does not come up the breathing should be repeated before trying to cough again, to avoid the continuous struggle already described. Special times should be set aside each day to concentrate on clearing the lungs; an odd cough now and then when they have become so full of mucus that some has to be removed to leave space for a little air, only gets rid of a tiny bit. The aim is to empty the lungs as nearly as possible of the mucus, because while there is any there more will be produced; mucus creates mucus rather like a ginger beer plant produces ginger beer. A controlled, concentrated period of coughing will remove large quantities of sputum leaving the lungs relatively clear and able to use the oxygen breathed in to advantage. They are very congested in the mornings so a period of coughing should precede getting up, with another at lunch time, and before going to bed. This last one at night will relieve tightness, discomfort and breathlessness and allow much more restful sleep.

The position adopted for coughing depends on the individual, though it is best to lie down on the bed. Ten minutes should be spent lying on one side before even starting to cough, the mucus can then drain out of the lungs and is easier to cough up. After clearing one side, ten minutes should be spent on the other before clearing that side too. Many people find it easier to cough sitting up, but if they can spend the time lying down first it will be much less of a strain.

Having cleared the lungs as much as possible, five minutes should be spent concentrating on breathing exercises to make them expand more fully and re-educate the breathing mechanism. As the breath is drawn *in* the lower ribs and the stomach should be pushed *out* to take the air right down to the bottom of the lungs. Most bronchitics breathe only with the very top of their chests, straining with the muscles of the neck and shoulders to get enough air. Long, slow breaths should be taken, not the shallow rapid breathing that makes bronchitics so short of breath. Placing the hands on the ribs helps one to appreciate the movement of the chest as the air is drawn in. This type of breathing should be practised regularly until it becomes automatic; it is no good being very good at it lying on the bed, but still panting the way down to the shops or the pub. When the body is active it needs more air, so correct breathing is doubly important (see chapter 14).

Keeping the lungs clear, the chest mobile and the breathing controlled, not only makes life much more comfortable and active, but helps to prevent further acute attacks and diminishes the strain on the heart.

8 Care of the feet and legs

Our feet work very hard indeed. They are subjected to abuse by ill-fitting shoes and obesity, and have to carry our entire weight wherever we go. As we become older they become smaller due to loss of fat, the skin becomes dry, and calluses form on pressure points. Nails thicken and become a source of infection, and the muscles maintaining the arches of the foot lose their tone causing ligaments to become strained.

Pain in the feet can usually be relieved, so there is very little need for anyone to hobble about in agony. A visit to the doctor and the chiropodist is essential, and the latter should be a regular appointment (see chapter 15).

Foot strain

If foot muscles become weak the weight is taken on the ligaments between the bones. This causes acute pain and inflammation, and very often swelling on the top of the foot, the ankle and the lower leg, although swelling in these areas may be caused by something else altogether.

Pain caused by some other reason such as chilblains or bunions can create stiffness and foot strain. Walking becomes difficult and the weight is taken through the wrong part of the foot in an effort to relieve it, at the same time upsetting the mechanism and straining the muscles and ligaments.

Hammer toes and bunions

Deformities of the toes do not usually cause pain in themselves, but become a source of pain if ignored or abused. A deformed toe or bunion is out of line with the rest of the foot and therefore becomes badly rubbed by the shoe. Both these deformities can be corrected by operation, but this is a fairly drastic measure and is often unsuitable for elderly people.

Temporary treatment for a bunion is to wedge a pad between the big toe and the second one to straighten them a little, and to find a pair of shoes that do not rub the affected place. An ordinary pair with holes cut in the appropriate places is the most satisfactory; it spoils the shoes but is better than being in constant pain. Sometimes a suitable pair of sandals can be found, but it is not a good idea to wear slippers. The chiropodist should be seen as soon as possible.

Calluses, ingrowing toenails and sore heels

Coarse patches of horny skin often develop on the areas of the feet that become rubbed by the shoes. The most common areas are the ball of the foot, the heel, and the bunion. If there are no open sores, soaking the feet in warm water and rubbing lanolin into the area will ease the pain by softening the hard skin, but it will not cure the problem. Do not try to cut the hard pieces away with a razor blade. It is rarely effective and is very likely to set up an infection. Instead, the chiropodist will treat the areas concerned, and also ingrowing toenails, which should not be cut in a haphazard way with scissors or blade. For the treatment of sore heels see chapter 11, section on bed sores.

Cramp

Cramp in the lower leg is common, particularly at night. The cause is unknown, but seems to be related to the limb being cold. Coldness and cramp are associated with poor circulation and can be helped by moving the feet up and down from the ankle, deep breathing also helps to encourage the blood to circulate freely. Occasionally it may be related to the recovery period after a stroke. In severe cases the doctor should be consulted, he can prescribe drugs which will ease the cramp, but in all cases increasing the circulation will help. Electric blankets create an even warmth, but as the 'under' type has to be turned off the 'over' type is more satisfactory and maintains an even warmth all night (see chapter 16, section on common sense and precautions). If a hot water bottle is used it must have a cover on it, and not be too hot, to avoid burns, particularly as coldness is often associated with defective sensation.

Varicose veins

Varicose veins are nearly always hereditary, though the condition can be aggravated by prolonged standing and habitual constipation.

The long veins of the legs, which carry the blood back to the heart, are supported by the muscles of the limb, and the contraction of the muscles aids the blood flow by a pumping action. Further help is also given by a series of valves situated in the walls of the veins which close across the vein to prevent the blood flowing back down the leg.

In the condition of varicose veins the muscles of the legs do not support the veins sufficiently to maintain a good flow of blood back up the leg; the blood tends to stagnate and the walls of the veins become lax and the valves inefficient. The legs ache and swell, and the poor circulation causes the skin to become patchy and thin, and to break down into an ulcer after the slightest knock (see leg ulcers p. 66).

There are several treatments for varicose veins, including an operation or having them injected. In both cases the vein is obliterated, and the blood flows through smaller collateral veins instead. Unless they cause a lot of pain and discomfort most elderly people would prefer to put up with them, but there are several measures that can ease the condition.

The flow of blood must be helped on its return to the heart by outside means, which include bandaging, elevation of the legs, and exercises. The legs should be raised on a stool, or on pillows while lying on the bed, to allow the fluid which has collected in the tissues to drain and the legs to return to their normal shape and size. This should be done at least twice a day for a period of half an hour each time. Before putting the legs down a bandage or elastic stocking should be applied (see below), and exercises carried out to strengthen the muscles and increase the circulation (see chapter 14).

Swollen legs and bandaging

Swelling of feet and legs is often an indication of a disorder in some other part of the body as well as a symptom of chronic foot strain, and varicose veins. Stroke patients may have a residual swelling due to disturbances in the nerve supply to the blood vessels. Some heart and kidney diseases are responsible for gross swelling and can be helped by drug therapy. Whatever the cause, it is important to resolve it as quickly as possible to avoid damage to the skin leading to ulceration.

First, visit the doctor, who will treat the underlying cause and give instructions for day-to-day management. Second, the instructions must be carried out exactly. Basically, they will include raising the end of the bed a few inches (but only if there is no heart condition), and not standing for long periods, or sitting for hours with the legs hanging down, when the fluid remains stagnated like the sediment at the bottom of a bottle. The feet should be raised on a stool and the circulation encouraged by pulling the feet up and down from the ankles (see chapter 14).

The most important local treatment is the use of a crêpe or elastic bandage, but it is very important that it is applied correctly. Badly applied bandages cause far more harm than good. It should be started at the base of the toes with a firm turn over the top of the foot, which is particularly prone to swelling.

Bandaging: showing first firm turn

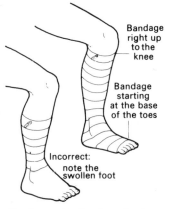

Bandage right up to the knee

Bandage starting at the base of the toes

Incorrect: note the swollen foot

Bandage extending from the toes to the knee

The bandage should be taut at each turn, so that it remains slightly on the stretch as it contacts the leg, and should cover half the previous turn. Particular attention should be paid to the area behind the ankle bones where fluid collects, and the whole bandage continued, *with even pressure*, all the way up the leg to the knee. *Never* start a bandage above the ankle, and *never* finish it below the level of the knee.

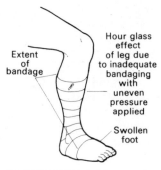

Hour-glass effect due to wrongly applied bandage

If there is an area with less pressure under it the fluid collects there and solidifies. When the bandage is removed the leg looks like a Venetian hour glass.

Remove the bandage at night, and reapply it every morning, *before* putting the feet out of bed on to the floor. Bandages lose their elasticity after a day or two of wearing, but it returns after washing in warm, soapy water. They should be dried flat, not hung on the line. Two bandages are necessary to allow them to be washed and dried properly; they will not dry overnight. Garters and stockings are not suitable for women with swollen legs as they restrict the circulation; suspenders must be used instead.

Many doctors prescribe elastic stockings, but unless they are made for the individual by a surgical fitter they are not very satisfactory. They are usually too tight round the calf and too loose round the ankle, unless the legs are exactly the shape the stockings were designed for. In spite of this, a well made bought pair are much better than nothing, and are useful for people who find applying a bandage difficult. Tubigrip, a uniform elastic tube which comes in a roll, is used a lot in hospitals but has the same drawbacks as bought stockings.

Leg ulcers

Ulceration of the lower leg is the result of poor circulation caused by small clots in the veins. The sluggish circulation is unable to keep the tissues supplied with the oxygen and nutrients necessary for healthy skin, which becomes devitalised and either breaks down of its own accord or is damaged by a slight knock. After the skin has broken the area will increase in size quite rapidly, while remaining very shallow, though in a few cases it becomes deeper rather than wider. The ulcer is accompanied by swelling in the lower leg and skin changes; it either becomes hard and tough, or papery and easily broken down still further. The combination of swelling and the skin condition causes stiffness and pain in the ankle and foot. These symptoms are due to the original circulatory condition rather than the ulcer itself.

There are several ways of treating ulcers and a visit to the doctor is essential. Many people just cover the ulcer up with a dressing and leave it, which causes infection and further breakdown. The doctor will decide what treatment is suitable, but it will include dressing by the district nurse and care of the whole lower leg. Management of swelling and instructions for bandaging are described in the previous section. Movement is particularly important and walking very beneficial, but standing should be avoided. If you are forced to stand in one place, tighten the calf muscles alternately, and raise the heels off the ground to make the calf muscles work and help to return the blood up the legs. Exercises which keep the foot and ankle mobile and increase the circulation are essential to the healing process, and should be practised at least three times a day; a stiff swollen foot with stagnant circulation will never allow an ulcer to heal. People with ulcers should never wear garters (see chapter 14).

9 Obesity and diet

Obesity Ten per cent of weight carried over the standard for a particular height is considered obese. Ten per cent is not very much but indicates that more calories are being consumed than are being used up. A calorie is a measure of heat which is normally burnt up by the exercise taken performing our daily activities, but if all the calories are not used they are stored in the body as fat.

Joints become worn out very rapidly when they have to take more weight than they were designed for; the feet, too, become chronically strained. Moving about is more difficult and requires more effort; even getting up from a chair becomes a struggle, and eventually may not be attempted. The effort required to perform the everyday tasks puts a tremendous strain on the heart and lungs, causing shortness of breath; obesity being a major factor in heart disease.

Overweight people should not sit in one place for a long time to save the trouble of moving. If they do, they risk becoming constipated and developing kidney and bladder disorders. Incontinence is fairly often traced back to this source (see Incontinence).

Overweight people are particularly prone to accidents; they seem to have less control over their movements than other people and are often top-heavy. High blood pressure can make them giddy, or an arthritic knee 'gives way', landing them with a terrific crash. After an accident there is the problem of nursing them, particularly if they are at home and have to be lifted about by a relative.

Diet Instead of cutting down on all foods indiscriminately it is better to understand which foods are useful to the body, and which are just fattening. Most people know that food is made up of carbohydrates, fats and proteins, minerals and vitamins. Carbohydrates are the fattening group and include potatoes, cakes and sweets. One problem is that people do not always realise how much they are eating. Many obese people say 'I only eat four pieces of bread for tea', or 'I do like a few potatoes' when they often have a huge pile of them.

Fats, too, although taken in smaller quantities, are fattening, but produce more energy for a longer period. Protein is the most important group as it contains necessary cell-building elements. Too little protein makes the continual process of replacing the cells which make up the body impossible to maintain. Vitamins and minerals are essential and are found in fruit, vegetables, meat and dairy produce.

A properly balanced diet taken in small regular meals can

make an enormous difference to the whole outlook on life. Malnutrition is not a thing that went out with the last century; it is fairly common among old people today. Although the gross intake of food may be substantial it is often largely bread and potatoes, and the foods that are high in essential protein and vitamins are never eaten. The financial situation is, of course, a very obvious reason for not eating properly, but it is possible to make nourishing meals on a small budget. A very good recipe book written by a dietician with old people in mind, is *Easy Cooking for One and Two* by Louise Davies, published by Penguin. Some areas run cookery classes for the over-60s, which are particularly useful for widowers. Meals on wheels can be arranged through the doctor or Social Services and ensure a good meal at least twice a week (see chapter 15).

Men, particularly, tend to live on bread and jam, and tea, or perhaps something out of a tin occasionally, and it is not always because they do not know how to cook; for those who have been married 'it doesn't seem worth it, just for one', is a common explanation. Often 'it doesn't seem worth it' because they have lost interest, or perhaps their dentures do not fit properly and eating is difficult. Sometimes they have no appetite and the food is tasteless, which may be a warning of underlying depression, or a disorder of the digestive system.

Joining a luncheon club or the Darby and Joan may help to regain contact after bereavement and stimulate the appetite by well presented food and cheerful company. For those who live with relatives, taking part in the preparation may help, as well as making them feel of some use.

Closely related to the problem of malnutrition, mentioned above, are mineral and vitamin deficiencies, which cause symptoms related directly to a lack of specific foods. Table 3 shows the main vitamins, the foods they are found in, and the symptoms caused by deficiency. It is not intended as a do-it-yourself diagnostic chart but to help in understanding why certain foods are necessary. If any of the symptoms mentioned are present the doctor should be consulted.

Halibut liver oil capsules and rosehip or blackcurrant syrup can be bought from the chemist and should be used throughout the winter. The WRVS supplies orange juice, dried milk, cod liver oil, Horlicks, Ovaltine, tea, Bovril, Marmite, and Complan at reduced prices from their local offices.

If large quantities of sugar are used in tea and coffee it should be replaced with Sweetex or saccharine tablets which can be bought from the chemist and are much cheaper than sugar.

Table 3	Vitamin	Source of food	Deficiency symptoms
	A	Dairy produce, halibut liver oil, fish, vegetables.	Night blindness (vision in dim light is poor), eye and skin infections.
	B	Milk, liver, yeast (Marmite, stout), lentils.	Skin irritations, sore eyes and tongue, cracks at the corners of the mouth, scaly greasy skin round the nose.
	C	Citrus fruits (oranges, grapefruit), tomatoes, green vegetables, watercress, blackcurrants, rosehip syrup, *new* potatoes.	Delay in healing of wounds, teeth become loose and gums sore, lowers resistance to infection, muscles become flabby. Vitamin C is low in smokers and rheumatoid arthritics.
	D	Milk, butter, eggs, cheese, liver, halibut liver oil.	Over-excitable nerves, softening of the bones.

Table 4	Fattening foods	Nourishing foods	
	Sugar	Meat	*New* potatoes
	Sweets	Chicken	Watercress
	Potatoes	Liver	Tomatoes
	Bread	Fish	Yoghurt
	Cakes	Eggs	Wholemeal or
	Puddings	Cheese	brown bread
	Pastry	Milk	Peanut butter
	Jam	Nuts	Marmite and Bovril
	Cream	Fruit	Complan
	Fried foods (grill instead)	Vegetables	Salads
	Thick soups and sauces		

Dehydration   Lack of fluid in the body is common in old people; many do not drink enough fluid deliberately, to avoid having to go to the lavatory; this is particularly so in hospital. Some are frightened of becoming incontinent, and many go without drinks quite inadvertently. Loss of fluid also occurs after vomiting or prolonged diarrhoea, which may give rise to a potassium deficiency in the diet, the symptoms of which are thirst, muscle weakness, confusion and general malaise. The doctor should be consulted and in the meantime liquids taken to replace the fluid and plenty of fruit eaten, which is high in potassium.

10 Incontinence and constipation

Incontinence of urine

One of the most distressing consequences of illness in old age is the indignity of incontinence, but with proper management it can either be kept under control or dealt with in a hygienic and not too unpleasant way.

The reason for lack of control is one of the prime factors in treating it. Diseases involving the brain cells, or the nerves to the bladder, cause the most difficult type of incontinence, that is, the lack of inhibitory control. Multiple sclerosis, stroke, and arteriosclerosis can interfere with the inhibitory impulses from the brain, though it is not inevitable that these illnesses will cause incontinence. It depends on the area of the brain affected. Lack of the control we learn at two or three years old makes the working of the bladder return to its original system of functioning, which is by reflex action. As soon as it is full enough to stimulate certain nerve endings situated in the lining, messages are sent to the brain which automatically make the bladder contract to empty its contents. This is, of course, very distressing as there is no warning at all. There is also very little hope of the condition improving except in the case of stroke patients, when, as I explained in chapter 3, the pressure put on the brain cells is gradually relieved as the blood is reabsorbed into the system, so that damaged cells controlling the bladder will recover and control be regained.

The best way to manage incontinence of this kind is to make sure that the bladder never fills enough to activate the reflex action which empties it. Regular visits to the lavatory every two hours are required, or if in bed, a bedpan should be given; better still the person should get out of bed on to a commode.

Reduced sensitivity of the emptying mechanism results in retention of urine, until the bladder is so full that it overflows in a constant trickle, the original urine still being in the bladder. This occurs most commonly in men with an enlarged prostate gland, and the full bladder can be felt through the abdominal wall. Sufferers can be taught to empty the bladder at regular intervals as with the previous group.

Another cause of incontinence is weakness of the pelvic floor, that is, the sheet of muscles forming the floor of the pelvis. These muscles are responsible for the control of the openings from the bladder, and the bowel. The bladder itself is quite normal but the muscular sphincters are weak and cannot hold the urine back, so the bladder empties if the person stands up, or coughs.

Control can be regained by re-education and strengthening of the muscles responsible. In extreme cases electrical stimulation of the muscles in the physiotherapy department is necessary, but for many people exercises combined with a renewed awareness can be very effective. The exercises should be performed for short periods several times a day (chapter 14).

Incontinence of this type is often encouraged by lack of movement, therefore walking around and general movement will help the muscles to start functioning again. It can also be a symptom of a prolapsed or 'dropped' womb which is caused by the failure of the muscles to regain their elasticity after childbirth.

Another physical cause for incontinence can be an infection in the urine which can be recognised by an unpleasant smell, and a burning sensation on passing water; sometimes there is a general feeling of being unwell and tiredness. It is fairly easily cleared up by antibiotics if it has not been left too long. Enlarged prostate and impacted faeces are space-filling complaints leaving less space for the bladder, which has to empty prematurely. Vaginitis causes irritation and discharge from the womb from which local inflammation can spread to the bladder, causing incontinence. Treatment from the doctor usually clears it up.

Apart from the physical causes, there are a number of psychological reasons for incontinence. It may be a protest against an unwelcome situation being imposed upon an old person, or a way of attracting attention if nothing else has the desired effect. Both these problems are difficult to manage; quite often the person may be unable to express what is troubling him or her, but kindness and understanding, combined with inclusion into the family life, are helpful.

In the case of the apparently wilfully incontinent an appeal to reason is sometimes effective unless the condition is due to laziness or confusion. If joints are painful, or the person is grossly overweight, it is often easier to wet the chair than to move. In these cases every practical assistance should be given: treatment from the doctor to help painful arthritis; the chair a suitable height to enable getting up without too much of a struggle; not having too far to go to the lavatory; and although fluids are essential, too many drinks should not be supplied unnecessarily. Elderly people in this group may be suffering from confusion and not realise the offence incontinence causes. They do not mind being difficult, but being cross about it will only make them more rebellious.

Anxiety and shame at being incontinent are common and normal in those who try hard to control it; patience and sympathy help, as well as clearing up the mess quickly, without a fuss, and then forgetting about it. Worrying will always make the situation worse, even in those who have given up the struggle and refuse to try very hard.

The more timid and fastidious old person is often made incontinent by the fear that she will not be able to get to the lavatory in time. This happens particularly in hospital when specific times are laid down for visits to the lavatory or the arrival of a bedpan; pleas in between times are frequently ignored by busy staff. An anxiety state is set up and results in a wet chair, or far more frequent requests to go; this turns into a crying wolf situation which nobody takes any notice of.

The key to managing incontinence is understanding and patience; understanding the reason why, and being patient with the trouble it causes. One of the worst discomforts in life is being at the mercy of one's bladder or bowels; but when one is old or ill one is also often at the mercy of the person with the bedpan or commode.

There are a number of general ways of helping to prevent or improve incontinence. The main one is to empty the bladder regularly every two hours. An old person needs to do this more often than a young one because their bladder shrinks slightly and loses some of its elasticity. This lack of elasticity can in itself cause trouble as it allows the bladder to become over-full, which in turn results in mental confusion, the same being true of constipation; but constipation may be the cause not the result of incontinence.

Sometimes when a bottle or bedpan is refused as soon as it is taken away the bladder empties. It is thought that the bottle or pan produces an inhibiting reflex which is released as soon as it is taken away. It is very trying for those who have to clear up, and embarrassing and worrying for the sufferer.

Exercise in the form of walking and moving about doing daily tasks helps to keep the kidneys and bowels working in a normal fashion, so walking to the lavatory rather than using a pan or commode is therapeutic in itself. Men who cannot reach the lavatory can have a bottle near at hand, but it should not be kept *in situ*, which causes infection and encourages laziness, no attempt at control being necessary.

The necessity to control incontinence is paramount in maintaining independence and general welfare. I have discussed the lack of control, but the incontinence itself has repercussions that are far-reaching. For the person sitting in a chair all day, or lying in bed, there is great danger of either producing bed sores or infecting sores already present. It is also very lowering for the morale and the dignity to be wet and smelly, quite apart from being most uncomfortable.

Management   If all attempts to cure the incontinence have failed, acceptance and practical management of the situation can help a lot towards making life easier. Regular emptying of the bladder saves enormous quantities of clothes and bed linen from having to be washed; if necessary gentle pressure on the lower abdomen will help expulsion. The doctor may prescribe tablets to inhibit the production of urine for a short period to save this procedure having to be carried out at night.

Bed clothes   Suitable clothes and bed linen save work. Protect the bed with a polythene sheet. A draw sheet under the hips helps to localise soiling when used with a plastic strip underneath it. An incontinence pad which is plastic on one side and absorbent material on the other, is invaluable, as it is thrown away; in some areas these are supplied through the Social Services. A fairly cheap one-way sheet called 'Marathon' is now available. Made in two sizes, it is non-absorbent, so that any wetness passes straight through to be absorbed by the draw sheet underneath, leaving the surface dry and comfortable. It is very thin and dries very quickly, making laundering easier. Many people will be familiar with babies' one-way nappies which are the same type of thing, and like them, the sheet can be cleaned and sterilised in a bucket with a nappy cleaner; they just need soaking for at least two hours and then rinsing thoroughly in cold water. In most areas the Social Services will arrange laundering of sheets in severe cases of incontinence (see chapter 15).

In chapter 11 I describe a specially prepared sheepskin which helps to prevent bed sores, though it is expensive. It is not as difficult to wash as one would expect.

Dress   Many clothes can be adapted for incontinent people, and should be made of easily washed materials that do not need ironing. Nightdresses and skirts can be made to open down the back with fasteners that can be easily undone, allowing the garment to be drawn aside before sitting down. It is not so easy to arrange for men, but at night they can go without pyjama bottoms, and in the day they must wear trousers made of terylene or nylon that can be washed overnight. For men and women a pad worn inside special plastic pants is added protection and is very useful for outings, or indeed all the time, but special care must be taken of the skin. Each time the pad is changed the skin should be thoroughly washed and dried before applying a barrier cream. This procedure is essential to prevent sores and urine rash, particularly if there is an infection in the urine.

Incontinence of faeces   Fortunately incontinence of faeces is much less common than incontinence of urine. The bowel mostly works automatically, and incontinence is caused by overfilling of the rectum which automatically expels its contents. The only way to control this is by regular enemas which prevent the bowel from becoming over-full. The district nurse may be asked to do this.

Another cause is impaction of faeces. The bowel becomes full of dry, hard faeces which cannot be expelled, and allows only fluid and loose stools to pass, so a condition that appears to be diarrhoea may be impaction. When this happens it is usually necessary for the person to be taken into hospital to have the obstruction removed.

Constipation   Constipation is a deviation from the normal bowel pattern for a given individual. Some people may pass a motion twice a day, others every two or three days. It is a very common complaint among elderly people, and is possibly due to a disturbance in the reflex action of the intestine. Old people eat less, and there is less bulk in the intestines to activate the expulsive reflex. The muscles of the abdominal wall and pelvic floor may be weak and interfere with the normal process. The exercises for the pelvic floor should be practised (see chapter 14).

Constipation may be the underlying cause of headaches, indigestion, wind, lassitude, and may cause the serious condition of impacted faeces (see above). There is a constant feeling of wanting to pass a motion which causes discomfort and pain, though fluid and loose stools can be passed.

Constipation should not be allowed to become a normal state of affairs, because apart from the discomfort and upset in the normal mechanism, it is a fairly common cause of mental confusion.

In ordinary cases, that is if there is no underlying medical condition, the bowel should be restored to normal movement by adopting a diet which is high in roughage: green vegetables, fruit and Allbran. As much exercise as possible should be taken, including tightening of the tummy muscles, and a renewed consciousness of the working of the intestines should be cultivated. The call to pass a motion should be answered immediately, not put off and forgotten.

Large doses of laxatives should be avoided except under doctor's orders, also Codein and Veganin which are very constipating. Some other drugs cause constipation as a side effect.

11 Care of the elderly person in bed

The dangers Old people, particularly if disabled, should not stay in bed unless they are ill enough for the doctor to be called. He will decide whether it is necessary, and for how long. A passing illness, such as bronchitis, or in the early stages after a stroke, are obvious examples of when staying in bed is necessary.

The old person himself may decide he cannot manage any more; rising and going about his business may not seem worth the effort, and this attitude is often accompanied by depression and apathy. Old people are very conscious of feeling cold and may stay in bed to keep warm, particularly if they are depressed or living alone. In some cases, especially those with obliging relatives, the reason may be laziness; it is much easier and more comfortable to be waited on in bed than to have to struggle to be active and independent. This is the sort of case that results in total inactivity on the part of the old person and exhaustion on the part of the relative. Many daughters and nieces are too tolerant and kind, and are taken in by pleas to stay in bed. Some are unable to assess the situation and give in to such announcements as 'I'm not getting up today'. They do not realise the implications of even a short stay in bed. The kindness that allows this is responsible for much disability and difficulty later on (see chapter 1).

For some relatives, of course, it is much easier for Mum or Dad to be in bed; they are out of the way and do not disrupt the running of the household. Sometimes this attitude is readily accepted as it is easy for both parties, but quite often it causes depression and a feeling of abandonment and loneliness. In the end the will to be independent is squashed and the old person complies with the restrictions imposed upon them. So the old person may provide one motive, the relatives the other.

Having been in bed a few days, for whatever reason, old joints become stiff and muscles weak, and when the time comes to get up the disabilities formed and the pain caused by them make it very difficult. Instead of recognizing the reason for the difficulties both the old people and the relatives think it is because they are not yet well enough to get up, or may even be getting worse, as they were quite well in that respect when they went to bed. So the stay in bed is prolonged. The stiffness makes movement difficult and painful so it is restricted, and soon turns into deformity and inertia. Nursing becomes a problem and in a very short time the few days in bed have stretched to the condition of being bed-ridden.

One old lady who had osteo-arthritis of the hips wrote in

response to my asking her how she felt about the fact that she had spent five years unnecessarily restricted to her bed and a wheelchair:

> Need I have been a cripple, attached to a wheelchair, for five years — No! No! No! After eventually being sent to hospital, and receiving treatment in the Physiotherapy Department I can now WALK!!! In the department I learned that I need not have been *lame* at all — it was really ·caused by excess love and kindness of my family — at first, when walking became painful, they put me to rest, when they should have gently exercised me, so that my joints could not become set, and a good circulation obtained — also I was fed too well, and my unnecessary weight made my walking much more difficult, I am now strictly dieting to have less weight for my legs to carry!!!

It sounds as if I have dictated it to her, but it shows that eventually she understood why she had been immobilised. During her period in hospital her daughter used to bring her chocolates 'to cheer her up'. She rightly pointed out that as she was eighteen stone and on a diet she should not eat them. The daughter's unhelpful reply was that she should eat them in the night when the nurses could not see.

Of course, for some people to remain active and mobile is impossible and in the last few weeks or months many must be looked after in bed, but this period should be made as short as possible by not going to bed before it is really necessary.

Problems of the bedfast

The trouble with being bedfast is that the situation does not remain static. Unless very expert nursing is employed the condition of the old person deteriorates as more problems arise, and even where full-time hospital care is available it is difficult to prevent them.

The first complication is the development of bed sores; a subject discussed in full at the end of the chapter. The deformities of the joints, particularly the knees and hips, become 'set' and irreversible; and the muscles continue to become weaker through debility and lack of use. The lack of movement enforced can lead to thrombosis, chest infections, loss of balance and incontinence (see chapter 10).

The other side of the problem shows worn out relatives trying conscientiously to do all they can. Even in the hands of experts it is difficult to stop a bedridden old person from deteriorating, so nursing at home cannot hope to maintain the situation, though thousands battle on very courageously, not wanting to give up and have their relative taken into hospital.

Management   If the situation arises, correct management and awareness of the problems can relieve many difficulties. Using the right equipment helps: a bed that is fairly high, about hip level, and free standing, not jammed up against the wall. If the bed has to be moved every time the sheets are changed or the patient turned, things are immediately much more difficult. The legs of the bed can be slotted into blocks in the same way as a chair is made higher (see chapter 16). If the bed is very soft an old door or some boards under the mattress will make turning much easier, and is better for the sick person.

The most important factor is movement, preferably initiated by the old person himself. If this is not possible it must be done for him, though if he is shown how he will probably help a lot. A rope over the bed will assist in turning, and moving up and down the bed.

General comfort is obviously of paramount importance. A cradle under the bedclothes takes the weight off the feet, enabling movement and avoiding the tendons on the front of the ankle becoming overstretched and useless. If the use of the cradle makes the feet cold, a small blanket can be wrapped loosely round them, or a warm pair of socks used. Cradles can be borrowed from the Red Cross.

Sitting on a sorbo pad covered with an old pillow slip to absorb perspiration can make all the difference in ensuring comfort, and it does help greatly to avoid bed sores of the sacrum and hips. Two rather expensive comforts are available which are extremely effective in reducing friction and pressure. A specially treated sheepskin under the hips, or used in a chair, is very luxurious and especially good for people who are incontinent, as it will absorb 33 per cent of its own weight in moisture without even feeling damp. For the prevention of sores nothing is better than a ripple bed; this is placed under the bottom sheet and consists of inflatable sections which are alternately blown up and let down by an electrically operated pump. To buy a ripple bed is very expensive but they can be hired fairly cheaply (see chapter 16). A piece of foam rubber tied to the elbows and heels with broad tape prevents friction from the sheets. It is important that the foam is over the area which takes the weight and that the tape does not cut into the skin.

Turning   If severe illness and disablement inhibits all movement and help from the sick person, great care must be taken in turning and positioning. Turning should take place every time attention is given to the old person to alternate the weight distribution between the back and each side (see bed sores, p. 86).

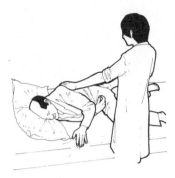

Turning an old person in bed

Even with a very heavy person turning should not be too difficult if it is approached correctly, and is very much easier if two people are available. Starting with the old person on his back: the head should be turned towards the helper, the arm brought across the body, and the far knee bent across the near thigh, then with one hand on the shoulder and one on the hip the body can be rolled over on to the side.

Some ill people feel that they are going to be rolled right off the bed, so the helper should stand close to the bed and re-assure them at the same time. If two helpers are present, the other one can slip her hands under the waist and the thighs and pull the hips into the middle of the bed, otherwise it is a matter of walking round the bed to do it.

To turn from the side onto the back the procedure is reversed. The arm and leg are moved towards the edge of the bed, the body rolled flat, and the hands then slipped underneath to pull the person back to the middle of the bed.

Lifting up the bed   If the sick person is to spend some time sitting up in bed, it is important that he is straight in order to prevent sores and deformity (see Positioning, p. 83). If he is ill enough to be permanently in bed he probably will not be able to sit himself up, which means he must be lifted, and unless it is done correctly it is very difficult and also a great strain on the helpers. The most important thing is to arrange the pillows so that they are nearly vertical and his seat can be sat well back. First of all, he should lean forward away from the pillows, which are then arranged; while still leaning forward the helpers grip hands behind his back and under his thighs and when he and the helpers are ready he is lifted right back against the base of the pillows (see chapter 13).

Bed changing and washing   Changing the sheets and giving the person a good wash can be done at the same time as turning, but before starting the room should be very warm. The easiest way to arrange the bed-clothes is to place a sheet which has been folded across four times on top of the normal sheet. It can be tucked in very near one end on one side and all the spare part in the other. If it is then only slightly soiled it can be pulled through instead of using a clean one. It can also be refolded to a clean piece on the top. While the sick person is turned towards the edge of the bed the draw sheet is rolled up and pushed under him.

Draw sheet rolled up and
pushed under the patient

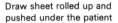

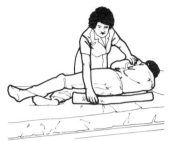

Changing the draw sheet

Giving a bedpan

Lying on the side

The clean one is spread in its place, the spare portion also being pushed underneath the dirty one. When he is rolled back, the dirty one can be pulled out quite easily and the clean one smoothed out and tucked in.

While he is lying on his side the opportunity can be taken to wash the back and clean up any soiled areas, and the sacral and shoulder areas can be massaged with spirit and glycerin (see Bed sores). Washing the rest of the body should be done in sections with only one part exposed at a time. Washing is a very personal thing and if possible he should be allowed to do it himself; if this is not practicable efforts should be made to cause as little embarrassment as possible.

If a bedpan is given about every two or three hours a lot of dirty linen can be saved. A bottle is easily used, but a bed pan can be more difficult. When the person is lying on his back, bend the knees and ask him to push on his feet and lift his seat off the bed; the pan can then be slipped underneath. For someone who cannot help at all two people are usually necessary; one stops the feet slipping while the other puts the pan under, as both lift the hips together.

If only one person is available and the bed is not too hard the sick person can be rolled onto it from side lying. Bedpans and bottles can be borrowed from the Red Cross.

Positioning   When an elderly person is very sick and in a debilitated condition the position in which he lies can make a big difference to his general comfort and the prevention of sores and deformities. The pillows should be as low as breathlessness allows; if he has a heart or chest condition the doctor should be consulted. Too many pillows causes a flexion deformity of the back and hips making the formation of sores more likely.

If the hips are stiff and the legs press together a piece of foam can be placed between the knees and ankles. Elbows and heels can be protected by foam also.

When the person is lying on his side he will probably be most comfortable with the underneath arm lying freely behind him, and the top knee bent up a little.

If he is allowed to sit up in bed the pillows must be arranged so that he sits up straight, not in a half and half position that puts all his weight through his sacrum and causes a sore very quickly. One firm pillow should be placed horizontally at the base of the headboard, two are then placed vertically, and the last one across the top. If they are very soft two may be necessary to support the head comfortably.

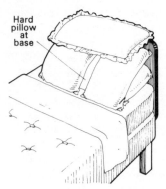

Hard pillow at base

Arrangement of pillows

If difficulties arise when nursing a sick person the Red Cross or the District Nurse can help by giving instruction or practical help in using the limited resources available in most homes, or contact the Home Nursing Department of the Area Health Authority.

Getting up again   When the time comes to get up, even if it is only to use the commode or to sit in a chair for an hour or so, the main problem will probably be fear (see chapter 6). A great deal of patience is needed and plenty of time; trying to hurry will fluster and frighten an already anxious person. It should be taken in steps so he feels that he has control of himself and the situation. Everything that is going to happen should be explained in detail, and the instructions repeated as they are carried out. It is a help to talk about it the day before so that there is time for adjustment. In general, proceed as explained on p. 99. Help should only be offered after an attempt has been made, not after the immediate 'I can't' which is so common, but is usually another way of saying 'I'm afraid'. The helpers should stand close by and be as reassuring as possible.

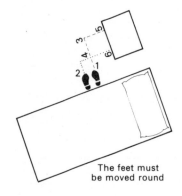

The feet must be moved round

The seat should not be swung round into the chair without moving the feet

Moving from bed to chair

This is quite an ordeal for many old people and the strong-minded, stubborn ones may well lie back and flatly refuse. In this case it is necessary to be firm, and as they are told to 'sit up', 'Put your legs over the edge of the bed', it may have to be done for them. They must not be allowed to think that they can stay in bed for that day, because exactly the same thing will happen each subsequent day. The main problem arising from this attitude is that when it comes to standing up the helpers may find themselves taking all the weight because the old person refuses to take it on his own legs and just lets his knees bend under him. If it is suspected that this may happen a third person standing by with a chair or stool can slip it underneath to prevent him falling on the floor, because if that is allowed to happen there will never be any hope of getting him to try again later.

This attitude of mind is often a basic cause of admission to hospital. It may arise from a battle of personalities within the family. Perhaps the elderly parent has always been dominant over the children and resents being told what to do. He or she also feels the indignity of not being as fit as hitherto and having to let their child do the everyday intimate things which they would normally do in private for themselves. On the other hand some say 'I have looked after my family all my life, now they are going to look after me'. Very often these problems are eliminated in hospital because although the physiotherapists and nurses may be half the age of the children at home they are wearing a uniform and the internal tensions of the family are excluded, though others may take their place, but they are easier to deal with if one is not emotionally involved.

This rebellious attitude can, of course, be caused by the approach of the relative or helper. Most old people are fairly frail and very sensitive where their own feelings are concerned. They get very worried and upset by being bullied or not receiving the sympathy they feel is their due, though this can be overdone and makes them very demanding. The attitude of the relative or helper is often reflected in the response, so if difficulties arise the approach should be examined before reproaching an innocent old person genuinely frightened or unable to perform the task in hand.

Sitting in a chair   Having successfully moved into the chair, the position taken up there is just as important as the position in bed, and for the same reasons (see p. 83).

Bed sores

Formation   Anyone who has spent a week in bed with flu will realise how quickly one develops a very sore behind. The formation of bed sores is caused by the weight of the body pressing the blood out of the area, combined with the stretching of the skin on the sheets. If the deep tissues are deprived of their blood supply they die, and the skin over the area breaks down. This process is more usual in old people as they change their position less frequently and the condition of the skin lacks the vitality of that of the young. The blood supply is sluggish and the skin less resilient, making the tissues more susceptible to breakdown. This over-all condition of lack of movement and lowered vitality also retards the healing process. If a young person cuts his finger it is completely healed in ten days, but if an old person gets a bed sore it may be ten weeks before it heals. If it is not treated expertly it will not heal at all.

The areas affected by pressure sores are those through which most of the body weight is distributed; unfortunately these coincide with the bony promontories. The most common areas to break down are the sacrum or 'tail' at the bottom of the back, the hips and heels. In addition to these areas the shoulder blades, elbows and ankles can be affected.

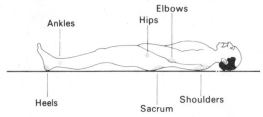

Pressure areas

I have already explained the action of reduced movement on the tissues, but there are other contributory factors which are equally important. Friction on the elbows and heels from pushing up the bed rapidly causes soreness and eventual breakdown of the skin. Dampness from incontinence not only encourages the formation of sores but causes infection once they are established. Bed sores also form in incontinent people after burns from acid urine.

It is quite possible for mobile people to develop sores, the most common example being those with arthritic hips. If the joints become stiff and will not bend sufficiently to allow them to sit upright in the chair the weight of the whole body is concentrated through the sacrum. Rising from the chair is difficult, which discourages getting up and walking around, thus producing conditions which predispose to the formation of the sore.

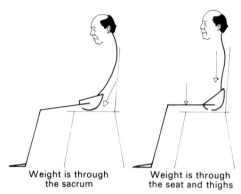

Weight is through
the sacrum

Weight is through
the seat and thighs

Incorrect sitting position puts
pressure on the sacrum

Prevention   Prevention of bed sores is the most important factor in nursing old people in bed. It can be a tremendous problem with the imperfect facilities of most homes, the lack of outside help and very often a heavy invalid.

The first sign that an area is under stress is slight reddening of the skin, so a constant watch should be kept. Movement and care of the skin are the two most important factors. Each time turning is in progress the opportunity should be taken to rub the danger areas. There are numerous lotions recommended for this purpose and most professional nurses have their own recipe; but a simple one, and a cheap one, is equal parts of surgical spirit and glycerin. A little is applied to the palm of the hand and rubbed over the susceptible areas. The hand must not skate over the skin as this produces the same effect as the friction of the bedclothes; slight pressure should be applied to help stimulate the circulation and move the top layers of tissue on those underneath, but massaging too hard grinds the skin on the bones beneath, creating ideal circumstances for the sore that is supposed to be prevented.

Pressure can be relieved to a certain extent by the use of a sorbo pad under the sacrum; if it cannot be borrowed from the Red Cross a sizeable piece can be bought fairly cheaply. Sheepskin rugs and ripple beds are very effective and are discussed in the previous section. For heels and elbows foam rubber is used as protection against the sheets.

The people who sit for long periods in a chair should choose one that is high enough to make getting up fairly easy, but not so high that their feet do not touch the ground, otherwise they are constantly slipping forward. They should sit with the seat well back in the chair and the thighs supporting the weight of the body; once the seat slips forward the whole body weight is concentrated through the sacrum and a sore forms. Sitting for a long time is also bad for the circulation which should be encouraged by frequent short walks, and while sitting, changing the position from one buttock to the other. Paralysed people are taught this and shift themselves every fifteen minutes. The use of a sorbo pad or sheepskin will also help, and a chair size ripple pad is made, but none of these things is a substitute for activity and good circulation.

Treatment   If bed sores develop it is advisable to call the doctor straight away, because treatment should begin on the very first day the skin breaks. There are many theories on their treatment ranging from applying honey to operating, though the latter is a fairly drastic measure. The doctor will probably arrange for the district nurse to do the dressings as it is necessary to act quickly once the skin has broken down, because the area will increase in size at an alarming rate, and if the person is very ill can become deep and extensive enough to expose the bone and ligaments of the sacrum. In the meantime turning should continue, leaving out the position in which the sore is involved, even greater attention being paid to the remaining areas.

If the sore is on the heel or ankle bone a four inch round piece of foam rubber about an inch and a half thick can be cut into a large corn plaster by cutting out the middle, and should be placed over the area. It can be kept in place by tapes or by putting it inside a large sock, and the whole foot kept off the bed by a pad placed behind the ankle.

Sacral sores in mobile people should also be dressed by the district nurse, and as much walking about as possible encouraged to increase the circulation and aid healing. Instead of sitting in the usual chair in which the sore was developed, an upright garden chair should be used instead; the type made of canvas with a gap at the bottom of the back. If the person is kept sitting upright in it the sacral area is not touched by the chair and no pressure is put on the affected area.

Attendance allowance   If an old person has needed full day-time or night-time attention for a period of six months the relatives are entitled to an allowance each week, which can be claimed from the Social Security Department (see chapter 15).

12 Changes in behaviour

Some elderly people seem to undergo changes in behaviour which create difficulties for themselves, and for the people with whom they are living. Their ability to adjust to alterations in their way of life is diminished. Bereavement, moving house or going into hospital can cause unhappiness and fear, and deafness or loss of sight contributes to old people becoming lonely and inward looking. Many people who live alone become saddened and unable to find any joy in life. Disabilities such as arthritis or heart disease make getting about more difficult and physical or mental isolation sometimes results. They see themselves becoming more disabled and lonely, and feel that no one cares about them (even some with good relatives feel this). They gradually withdraw from life outside and become even more isolated.

Listlessness, lack of initiative, fear of the future and anxiety about minute details of order and tidiness, combined with insomnia, characterised by waking in the small hours of the morning, may be early signs of depression. The disability and pain caused by arthritis or other illness may become exaggerated into fear of some more serious disease. Sometimes symptoms of other illnesses present themselves which are very real to the sufferer and are occasionally interpreted as retribution for past sins. A deep sense of guilt is common in people who are depressed; they lose weight which confirms their fears, but the cause is often that they are not eating properly. Fear of retribution often creates conflict as many depressed people think of dying as a release from their unhappiness.

When depression is secondary to another disability such as a stroke, or fractured 'hip' there is often preoccupation with constipation and fear of wanting to go to the lavatory when it is not convenient. It is common, too, to find those who think that others are doing their best to keep them immobile, or the opposite, when they blame themselves for the mess they are in and see no future worth getting better for.

Living with a depressed person can be very difficult indeed. Obviously one wants to try and help them, but all efforts to explain away their problems are fruitless. They will not be reassured, and are convinced that nobody can possibly understand them. The most practical thing to do is to make them as physically comfortable as possible, and to try to make them feel loved and part of the family, by reassurance and by bringing them into the general conversation. In time, and with the help of treatment from the doctor, they may begin to feel less hopeless.

In some old people the memory becomes impaired, particularly in relation to recent events. Although long-term memory is usually excellent the assimilation of new facts may be difficult, which can make readjustments a problem. A bereavement resulting in a move to a relative's home may cause complete disruption of mental stability. Friends may not be recognised and everyday tasks cannot be performed in the new surroundings. The ability to learn new tasks or take in new facts is affected in spite of being given extra time in which to perform them, and concentration for any length of time is impossible. This lack of concentration is completely unconscious, and instead of not going out because a person knows he will not remember the way home, he does not go because he has lost the desire to venture out. It is a protective reflex; anyone recovering from a bad back will know that they just do not want to dig the garden or move furniture, perhaps only realising why after the decision has been made. In the elderly the situation tends to snowball as each activity that needs some concentration or mental effort is pushed out of the way, until ultimately life progresses in an ever more restricted routine.

If the memory deteriorates insomnia may become a problem, when people walk about at night as if it was lunch time. The reason for this is that loss of memory has taken a particular form in which the normal patterns of each day are forgotten. Although it is normal to find loss of memory in old people there comes a point where it becomes incapacitating. In most of our lives each day of the week is made up of activities peculiar to it; perhaps meals on wheels comes on a Monday, or on Tuesday it is Darby and Joan and so on. If someone does not remember that the shops are shut on a Sunday there is no reason for not going down the road for some bread; there is also nothing to tell them that it is Monday until meals on wheels arrives, but then it probably comes on Thursday too, so there is further uncertainty.

One of the most difficult problems is avoiding accidents, because although old people do not mean to be awkward, or as it sometimes appears, maliciously mischievous, they just do not remember that pulling the bottom plate out from under a pile will make the rest fall on the floor, or combined with loss of table manners, that tipping food onto the floor is messy and offensive to other people.

It is fairly common for old people to show a reduction in emotional response, and lessening of social conscience may result in unacceptable behaviour. They may become slovenly, loss of dignity making them care little for the refinements of clean clothes, and there may be slackness in general hygiene. Those people who show these traits are often aggressive or even abusive and show irritation and jealousy towards other members of the family.

Being irritable and suspicious of others is fairly common in people who are blind or deaf. Many people discuss a deaf person secure in the knowledge that they cannot be heard, but it is usually obvious to the victim, who may start suspecting that all speech is directed against him. Similarly blind people often think that things are being put out of their reach, or have been hidden from them. Some people think that others are constantly plotting against them and they are surrounded by a fear of impending disaster. They feel lonely and think everyone hates them. Their delusions are usually very detailed and complicated, sometimes relating back to events in earlier life. They often dread the thought of being old and resent younger people who are healthy and happy, which can be very difficult if they are living with a daughter or a niece.

It is fairly common for old people to develop an unnatural regard for some possession such as a handbag or pipe, or to perform a particular ritual such as washing the hands or combing the hair, or even a trivial activity such as twisting the corner of a sheet. Some people are convinced that their belongings are being tampered with or that someone else is wearing their clothes. Most obsessions are fairly harmless and can be humoured without much trouble. People in this condition may well worry about being a nuisance to others, or that they cannot cope with looking after themselves. They tend to be agitated, and fear of certain activities may develop, particularly of walking. They feel uncertain and frightened of falling over, which makes them grab onto the furniture. The legs become unstable and the knees give suddenly, and although this rarely results in a fall it is painful and frightening. The fear of walking produces a rigid posture with the weight thrown back onto the heels, and the hands holding tightly onto a walking frame or stick (see chapter 6). Tremendous patience and perseverance are needed to help such people; they must have confidence (as far as that is possible) in the people who are helping them to walk, and must not experience even the slightest doubt that they may be let down. It is useless in most cases to find a good reason why they should not be frightened because the importance attached to walking makes them even more anxious.

Anxiety can sometimes produce incontinence, and may be a protest against some real or imagined injustice. There is a preoccupation with going to the lavatory and they ask to be taken constantly. In some cases there is a good medical reason why they feel as if they want to go all the time, but whether it is real or imagined it feels just the same. I am sure most people have experienced similar situations of knowing there is no lavatory within miles, and as soon as the fact has registered feel they must go at once (see chapter 10).

It is easy for the relatives of the very old or disabled to become over-protective. Those who are bedfast or disabled for a long time become so used to being told what to do, and when and how to do it, that eventually they become unable or unwilling to think for themselves at all. They are old and tired and it is easier to let someone else do the thinking for them. They are constantly asking questions such as 'Shall I get up?', 'Shall I sit down?', even 'Which foot shall I start walking with first?', and so on all through the day. To these types of question I usually say 'What do you think?' and so a decision has to be made. Old people at home should be encouraged to decide which clothes they are going to wear, and when they are going to get up or go to bed, otherwise they gradually lose all interest in social and family affairs and live their lives, or rather have them lived for them, in a boring routine pattern.

A serious problem arises concerning the future, or money, when they are suddenly expected to make major decisions, but are quite incapable of doing so. They become frightened and non-committal and end up with somebody else making the decision for them whether they like it or not. This situation is often made worse by relatives being too kind and doing too much.

Confusion is usually a temporary condition. It is described as 'a disordered awareness of environment'. Acute pain, or a sudden disturbance such as a stroke or an acute chest infection, may be responsible for confusion. If the medical reason is discovered and treated the condition will subside and the old person return to normal.

A chronic type of confusion is also found in the elderly and may show some of the behavioural changes that have already been described. No amount of reasoning or understanding will change them, so just encourage them, remind them of recent events, and try to stimulate interest in the present. If they become agitated and worried about hallucinations, let them see that someone is concerned and trying to ease the situation for them, while in fact distracting them to some other train of thought, though this can be difficult. Some old people wander about and can cause a lot of worry to others and danger to themselves. When they are going somewhere, which to them is usually very definite, like going to catch a train, take their arm and suggest going to see them off. By the time they have been redirected back to where they were, if they have not forgotten where they were going, the chair in which they will sit can temporarily become a train seat. It is useless to try to convince them that they are not going to catch a train because they become very upset and an unpleasant row ensues.

Younger relatives should try to be very patient when the elderly members of the family are 'difficult' because there is usually a reason for the behaviour. It is important not to be irritated into speaking harshly because the behaviour that is unacceptable will be consciously exaggerated in protest. Most old people with behavioural changes have no idea that they are distressing in the first place, and it seems as if they are being attacked for some unknown reason. Those people who are doing most for them and probably care for them more than other people must get used to being under attack.

If the behaviour of elderly people becomes too difficult to manage at home, or becomes a danger to themselves or others around them, the doctor can arrange for admission to hospital for a while. It helps to stabilise the old person and also gives the young ones a rest.

13 Daily activities

There are many activities we all perform every day without thinking about them, such as getting in and out of bed, going upstairs or getting out of a chair. If through disability these simple activities become major obstacles to normal living, they can be made very much easier, and safer, by doing them in a specific way. The instructions should be followed closely.

Sitting down in a chair

Walk right up to the chair. Many people try to reach it from too far away and fall over. *Turn right round* so that the back is to the chair, and *step backwards* until the back of the legs touch it. Turn slightly round to look for the arm of the chair, then let go of the walking aid, or put the sticks to one side and *put the hands on the arms of the chair.* Lower the seat *slowly* into the *back* of the chair by letting the knees bend, and by bending the body forward from the waist. If your seat ends up too far forward in the chair, lean forward and push with the hands on the arms of the chair and lift your seat back.

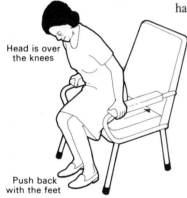

Head is over the knees

Push back with the feet

Moving back in the chair

Stiff hips

If one hip is very stiff the weight must be lowered onto one side only, keeping the stiff leg out in front. If both are affected the weight must be taken on the arms and the body lowered into the chair with the hips straight and the knees bent.

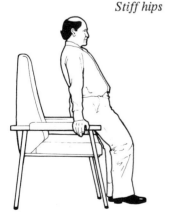

Sitting down with stiff hips

Sitting in a chair

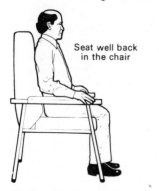

Seat well back
in the chair

Sitting correctly in a chair

The seat should be well back in the chair with the body upright and the weight on the thighs not on the base of the spine (see Bed sores in chapter 11). The feet should be squarely on the floor; crossing the legs encourages deformity in the hips, and spasm in stroke patients.

Stroke

The thighs must take the weight squarely, many people with a stroke sit only on the good side, which retards recovery. Spasm can be relieved by putting weight through the part, therefore sitting firmly reduces the spasm in the seat and side.

Slipping forward

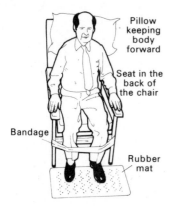

Pillow
keeping
body
forward

Seat in the
back of
the chair

Bandage

Rubber
mat

The use of a bandage and rubber mat prevents slipping forward in the chair

Very ill people, or those whose balance is disorientated, tend to slip forward out of the chair (see chapter 6). The old person should sit correctly as described above. Place a pillow behind the shoulders to keep the top half of the body forward. Put a Rubbermaid mat on the floor to prevent the feet slipping and if this does not prove sufficient, tie a bandage across the front legs of the chair to keep the legs back. Care must be taken that the bandage does not cut into the shins. If the knees and hips can be kept at right angles the seat is prevented from slipping forward.

Confusion

A confused old person is usually quite capable of sitting in a chair but is prone to wandering about and getting into trouble. If this happens the best thing to do is to place a low table in front of him with something interesting on it for him to do, and tie the legs of the table to the chair so it cannot be pushed away. It is important not to leave anyone long enough to get bored, and to take notice of them rather than getting them settled and then going away and forgetting about them.

Standing up from a chair   First of all the chair must not be too low; if it is, use blocks to raise the height (see chapter 16) or use another chair. *Slide the seat forward* to the edge of the chair, *bend the feet back under it*, and lean the *body forward* so that the head is over the knees. *Put the hands on the arms of the chair*, not on the walking aid, and *push upwards and forwards* with the arms, while pushing on the legs at the same time. If a stick or frame is used it should be placed ready, and the hands transferred from the chair to the aid after standing up with the legs quite straight.

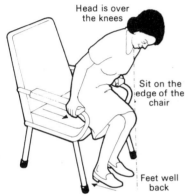

Head is over the knees

Sit on the edge of the chair

Feet well back

Getting up from a chair

Stroke   Make sure the weak leg is bent with the good one; many people try to get up with the leg stuck out in front of them, which pushes them back into the chair each time they try to get up.

Stiff hips   People with strong arms can lift their seat off the chair and 'walk' the hands forward along the arms of the chair while pulling the legs back underneath them. It is difficult to do this because there is no flexion at the hips, but the higher the chair the better. If the arms are weak a chair with a tip-up seat can be used, which raises the body high enough to enable most people to rise fairly easily (see chapter 16).

Getting into bed   Although it is easier for a helper to have the bed away from the wall to enable easy access on both sides, many old people feel much more secure if there is a wall there to prevent them rolling out on the other side. For the majority of people it does not matter which side they get in, but for stroke victims it does. The ease with which anybody gets in and out of bed depends on the height; it must be low enough to sit on to get in, and high enough to make getting up off the edge fairly

Sitting up by the pillows

easy. The most satisfactory height is about two feet, depending a little on the size of the occupant. If the old person can do very little for himself and a lot of help is needed it is easier to have the bed a little on the high side to prevent the helper hurting her back while lifting and bed-making. As when sitting in a chair, it is very important to get really close to the bed before letting go of the frame or stick and sitting on the edge of the bed. It is important to *sit right up by the pillows* to avoid having to struggle up the bed once in it.

Having sat down, the legs are lifted up onto the bed, and taking the weight on the hands the body moved into the middle of the bed, and if necessary up towards the pillows.

Stroke   If the disability is not too incapacitating and the person can get in and out of bed by himself, and also move around fairly easily in bed, it is more convenient to have the good side away from the wall so he can reach his belongings on the bedside table. If help is needed for all these things the weak side must be away from the wall to allow a helper to lift the paralysed side, and to provide adequate support while getting in and out of bed. In this case, if there is no room for a bedside table, perhaps a shelf could be put up on the wall to take his belongings.

The weak leg can be helped up onto the bed by slipping the good one underneath it and moving the two together. Beginning in the correct place, up by the pillows, is particularly important as it is difficult for people with a stroke to lift themselves up the bed.

Moving up the bed

Body leaning forward

Seat lifted back towards pillows

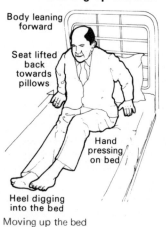

Hand pressing on bed

Heel digging into the bed

Moving up the bed

People who lie in bed need to pull themselves up to readjust their position and make themselves comfortable, and moving up the bed seems to cause a great deal of trouble for many disabled people. The first thing to do is to *sit forward* away from the pillows, and support the body with the hands on the bed. The knee is bent up and the heel dug into the bed as the *seat is lifted on the hands* and moved back up the bed.

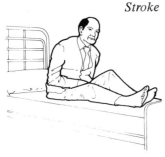

Stroke: moving up the bed

Stroke This is a difficult manoeuvre for people who have had a stroke because they fall towards the weak side. The same method is used except all the weight is leaned over on to the good side and must be taken on the good hand while the leg on that side pushes the body up the bed. If the stroke side is very weak it will be necessary to have some help. All that is required of the helper is that she takes the weight of the leg with one hand, and puts the other under the arm to prevent the body falling to that side while the person does the rest as described above.

Many people are helped a great deal by the use of a monkey rope hanging from the ceiling which enables them to pull themselves up the bed by lifting themselves with it (see chapter 16).

Painful shoulders Moving up the bed is very difficult if the arms cannot be used to take the weight of the body. While actually getting onto the bed special care must be taken to sit right up by the pillows, and as the legs are lifted up onto the bed the *body must be kept leaning forward* to prevent the hips slipping down away from the pillows. A cradle in the bed with a board slipped through it to support the feet will help to prevent slipping down, and a monkey rope may be of some use. Some people find they can pull on the rope when they cannot push up on the bed.

Getting out of bed

There are two ways of getting out of bed and most people can manage one or the other, but before even beginning the walking aid or sticks should be placed ready and within reach to be used as soon as the person is up. The first way depends largely on the strength of the stomach muscles. The body is brought up into sitting by using those muscles and by *pushing on the bed with the hands*. Once in the sitting position the legs are moved to the edge of the bed and are lowered over the edge. A pause should be taken at this point to prevent the change of position causing giddiness, before sliding off the bed to stand on the floor and take hold of the walking aid or sticks.

The other way is suitable for people with a stroke who have their weak side away from the wall, and those with backache. It is in fact the 'correct' way. While lying down, *turn onto the side* facing away from the wall, put the legs over the edge of the bed and *push the body upright* by pushing with the top hand on the bed in front of the chest.

Getting out of bed

Dressing   It is safer and easier to dress while sitting down, and many old people find it simpler to put most of their clothes on while sitting on the edge of the bed. It is usually a fairly prolonged activity so the room should be adequately heated. The top things can all be put on before starting on the bottom half, and most of them, too, before there is any need to stand up at all. See pp. 40–1 for details of how to go about dressing, and also chapter 16. At the end of the chapter on *Stroke* I have given advice on special problems arising from this condition, but it may be of use to other people too.

Getting up off the floor   Fear of falling over is one of the most restricting factors in the elderly, and justifiably so. Even if they get away without a serious injury it is a very disturbing experience which creates severe shock and an even greater fear of falling in the future. A great many falls can be prevented (see chapter 6). I have also explained how to get up off the floor, and how to attract attention if unable to get up (pp. 58–9). See also 'Lifting' at the end of this chapter.

Walking up and down stairs   When stairs become difficult, or frightening, the problem can be solved in the majority of cases by bringing the bed downstairs; it may be necessary to use a commode or elsan as well if the lavatory is upstairs, but it is preferable to a serious fall. Even if stairs are not involved in the home they are bound to be encountered at some time, and are not as difficult as may be supposed. The general rule is to *go up with the good foot first*, and *down with the bad foot first*. Each step should be taken separately so the same foot leads each time. The strongest leg should take the strain and body weight whether going up or down. The good foot is used to go up because it

Down with
the bad foot

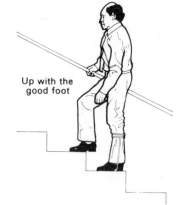

Up with the
good foot

Walking up and down stairs

must raise the whole person up onto the next step which requires a good deal of strength. Coming down needs a lot of concentration because the natural thing seems to be to lead with the good foot again, but it is the back leg which takes the strain while the front one is put down on the step below with the knee straight, and the vulnerable half-bent position avoided.

It is not wise to let giddy or very weak people negotiate stairs on their own, but with a little support under the arm to steady them and give confidence most people can manage. Of course the banister must be used and if possible another should be put on the other side as well, or at least a firm piece of rope.

Helping the elderly to walk

The most important thing is *not to help too much*. However weak and unsteady someone is they have a natural balance and pattern of moving, even if it does look ungainly and often unsafe. By helping too much the remaining part of these natural aids are unable to work for themselves and leave the person in a state of total imbalance. It is rather like doing a three-legged race with a partner one is not 'in tune' with, or trying to ride a tricycle again after being used to a bicycle. It is common to see relatives clutching onto an arm or encircling the waist in an effort to help, when all they are doing is taking away that vital natural balance and trying to impose their own. Within reason, however disabled an elderly person is, a firm hand held under the arm, plus the use of a walking aid to give confidence and take most of the weight, is all that is needed. If the situation arises when this is not enough, it is necessary for someone else to be on the other side. It is possible to feel how much help to give if the helper is sensitive to the walker's balance rather than his own. If a stick is being used the helper should stand on the opposite side to it, if an aid, he should stand on the side of the arthritic leg or painful foot. In most cases, if only one stick is necessary it should be used on the opposite side to the affected leg.

Lifting

One of the aims of this book is to help old people do things for themselves, so that lifting and heavy nursing are unnecessary, but inevitably they will have to be done sometimes for some people. The main lifting problems are lifting up the bed, and getting someone off the floor. They require two people. There are two methods of lifting up the bed; the first one is suitable for old people with fairly strong arms and is more comfortable for them and easier for the lifters. First of all sit him forward and rearrange the pillows so that they form a vertical back rest. When ready the lifters face the pillows, put

one arm under the knees and grasp each other's hand; then bend forward and put the shoulder nearest the person under his arm so it is lying down the lifter's back. The lifter's free hand is on the bed to take the strain. When everyone is ready, particularly the elderly person, lift exactly together and move the seat right up against the base of the pillows.

Lifting an old person up the bed
(method 1)

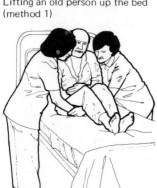

Lifting an old person up the bed
(method 2)

The second method is more straightforward. Having sat him up, face him, link hands under the knees, and behind the back, and lift back against the pillows as before.

If a piece of furniture is not near
enough, the feet are prevented
from slipping by the lifters' feet

Lifting someone off the floor

Lifting a heavy old person off the floor is no easy matter. If possible move him so he is facing a wall, a firm piece of furniture, or something that will prevent his feet from slipping. Have a chair within reach. Sit the old person close up to the wall so his knees are bent; the lifters should face him and put the arm nearest him under his and their feet one in front of the other.

When ready swing him up onto his feet and slip the chair behind him. If he can help by holding his arms down firmly and pushing with his legs so much the better.

If the old person is very weak and floppy put a belt round the waist, which can be held onto at the back to take the body weight.

Note   An old person should only be moved off the floor if no injury has been sustained. If he is unconscious or has pain in any part of him he should be laid as flat as possible and made comfortable while the doctor is called.

14 **Exercises**

Throughout this book I have stressed the importance of keeping the muscles strong and the joints mobile. I shall tabulate the exercises for each part of the body indicating the conditions for which they are most useful. The positions indicated for each exercise are important because they enable it to be performed most efficiently. The number of times each exercise is carried out is less important than the full range of movement achieved; three or four useful exercises are better than twenty that do not increase the range or strengthen the muscles at all. If in doubt as to how far a movement should go it can be compared with the opposite side, or, if that is not normal either, with a friend or relative who is. Each movement should be taken as far as the joint will go and then an extra effort made to make it go a little further. Many stiff joints will be fairly painful but this should be put up with to a certain extent; the only exception to this being those affected by rheumatoid arthritis.

Similarly with the exercises for strengthening muscles; they should be tightened as hard as possible, and then the extra effort made to make them even harder. If the joint is moved within the range it can already perform, or the muscle only made to work as hard as it easily can, no progress will be made; it is the effort beyond the normal that counts. For the majority of complaints the more often and the more concentrated the effort, the better are the results. At least twice a day time should be set aside for the exercises, but they can also be done at odd times as well. Several of the exercises can be done while sitting down having a cup of tea or while watching television, particularly hand and foot exercises, and those for strengthening the thigh muscles. The latter can easily be done by putting the feet up on a stool and lifting the legs now and then; quite a good number could be done during the course of one programme. The same is true for those people who have swollen legs and feet. It is an excellent opportunity to reduce the swelling by keeping the legs up and doing the foot and ankle movements described.

Many people will have been attending the hospital for physiotherapy treatment for their various conditions, and will have been given exercises to do at home. It is important to do them; the physiotherapist can guide and help, but two or three half-hour treatments a week are not sufficient on their own and must be backed up by co-operation in practising the exercises at home.

Exercises

Feet and ankles

Exercises suitable for foot strain, swollen feet and legs, cramp, leg ulcers, and stroke (see chapter 8).

(a) Sit with the knees crossed.

    i   Pull the foot up and down from the ankle; when pushing down point the toes hard towards the floor. 20 times. Repeat with the other foot.

    ii Circle the foot round from the ankle drawing a large circle in the air with the big toe. 10 times. Repeat with the other foot.

(b) Sit with both feet flat on the floor, knees at a right angle.

    i   Keeping the balls of the feet on the ground raise the heels as high as possible; the top of the foot should be almost vertical each time. 10 times.

    ii Press the toes flat against the floor and while keeping them straight raise the ball of the foot off the ground to make a bridge. (This is a small movement but is important in re-educating the small 'sling' muscles supporting the arches of the foot.) 10 times. Repeat with the other foot.

(c) Lying on the bed with the legs raised on pillows.

    i   Pull the feet up and down from the ankle, alternately in a pedalling motion. Particular care should be taken to push right down, making the calf muscles work strongly to create a pumping action which helps to drain fluid out of the feet and legs. Keep the legs up for half an hour. This exercise can also be done while sitting down during the day with feet up on a stool.

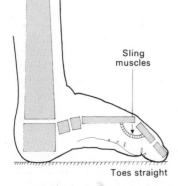

Sling muscles

Toes straight

Re-education of 'sling' muscles

Knees

Exercises suitable for osteo-arthritis, rheumatoid arthritis, stroke, Parkinson's Disease, fractured 'hip', unsteadiness, and knees that 'give way'.

(a) Sit with the legs out straight on a stool, or sit on the bed.

    i   Brace the knees back by tightening the thigh muscles. The back of the knees should be pushed against the stool or bed. Keep them tight for a minute, then relax. Tighten really hard and relax. 20 times with each leg.

    ii Brace the knees back as before, and when the muscles are really tight lift one leg off the stool keeping the whole leg quite straight. It is only necessary to lift about a foot off the stool before putting it *slowly* down. The whole point of the exercise is lost if the knee is allowed to bend at any point. 10 times with each leg, increasing the number as the strength grows.

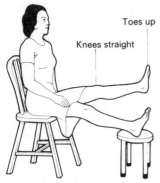

Toes up

Knees straight

Lifting the leg

iii   Bend the knees alternately to bring the heel as close to the buttock as possible. 10 times with each leg.

Hips   Exercises suitable for arthritis of the hips, fractured 'hip', Parkinson's Disease, stroke.
(a) Lying on your side on the bed.
    i   With the uppermost leg straight lift it up in the air about a foot, and bring it *slowly* down onto the other. 10 times. Turn over and repeat with the other leg.
(b) Sitting up on the bed.
    i   Bend one knee up onto the chest. If necessary put the hands round the knee and give a sustained pull. 5 times with each leg.
(c) Standing, holding on to the back of a chair.
    i   Facing the chair, swing the affected leg sideways as far as possible. A special effort must be made to keep the supporting leg straight, and the body upright. It is easy to allow the whole body to lean away from the affected leg, which results in the movement taking place in the back and good hip, while the other does not move at all. 10 times.
    ii   Standing sideways to the chair, swing the affected leg forwards and backwards, again, keeping the body upright to avoid movement in the wrong place. The backward movement is very important and helps to maintain a normal gait. 10 times.

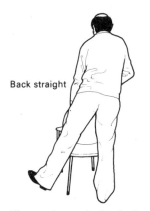

Back straight

Hip exercises: swinging the leg sideways

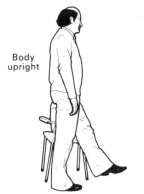

Body upright

Body upright

Movement in the hip not the back

Hip exercises: swinging the leg forwards and backwards

(d) Sitting on an upright chair.
    i   Bend forward to put the head as near the knees as possible. 10 times.

Note   Do not do this exercise if it causes giddiness.

Shoulders Exercises suitable for stroke, fractured upper arm, rheumatoid arthritis, and arthritis of the shoulder joint. The last three conditions should not be exercised in the very acute stage.

(a) Sitting on an upright chair which has no arms.

    i Let the arm hang down by the side and swing it forwards and backwards in a pendular movement. 5 times to begin with, increasing to 20 times.

    ii With the arm hanging as before swing it away from the side. 5 times increasing daily to 20 times.

    iii Supporting the hand and wrist, raise the elbow away from the side. 5 times increasing daily to 20 times.

    iv With the hand on the lap try to lift it up to the mouth as if eating. 10 times.

    v Lift the arm up to place the hand behind the neck as if combing the back of the hair. 5 times.

    vi Place the hand behind the back and try to reach up to the shoulder blades. 5 times.

    vii Lift the arm right up above the head as if reaching a shelf. If this is difficult at first, help it a little by supporting the wrist with the good hand. This exercise is particularly important in preventing a painful shoulder in people who have had a stroke.

(a) Away from the side   (b) Over the head

Raising the arm

Wrists and hands Exercises suitable for fractured wrist, osteo- and rheumatoid arthritis of the hands, and stroke.

(a) Sitting in a chair.

    i Make a fist with the fingers, and then straighten them out as far as possible. Repeat with each hand. 20 times.

    ii With the fingers straight spread them out to make wide spaces between each. 20 times.

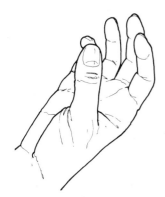

Hand exercises for grasping
muscles and dexterity

iii With the palm uppermost, take the thumb across to
the tip of the little finger, run the thumb down to the
base. Repeat with each other finger. 5 times.
iv   Circle the thumb round in large rings. 10 times.
v   Holding the elbow in to the side move the hand up
and down from the wrist. 10 times.
vi   Keeping the elbow in, circle the hand round in large
circles. Unless the elbow is kept in, the movement
occurs at the shoulder and not the wrist. 10 times.
vii Holding a stick about the width of a walking stick,
grip it tightly, and relax the grip. 10 times. Using a
cloth or piece of washing wring the water out getting
it as dry as possible. Doing some hand washing is excellent exercise after the plaster is taken off after a
fractured wrist, but heavy articles such as towels
should be avoided for a while.

Neck   Exercises suitable for osteo-arthritis, Parkinson's Disease, and
bronchitis.
(a) Sitting on an upright chair.
i   Move the head forwards and back, the backward
movement being very important, particularly for
those with Parkinson's disease. 5 times slowly.
ii   Circle the head round making it go as far as possible in
each direction. 5 times, slowly.

Note   Exercises for the neck can make some people giddy and should
be performed very slowly. If any giddiness occurs they should
be discontinued.

Back   Exercises suitable for bronchitis, Parkinson's Disease, and
'backward tilt'. (People with 'backward tilt' should only do
the forward bending exercises. See chapter 6.)
(a) Lying as flat as possible on the bed.
i   Press the head and shoulders hard back into the bed.
Relax, and repeat 10 times.
ii   Using the tummy muscles. Lift the head up to look at
the feet. 10 times.
(b) Sitting on an upright chair.
i   Put the head back and arch the back while taking a
deep breath in. Relax and breathe out. Repeat slowly
5 times.
ii   Sitting up straight, twist the body round to look behind, keeping the seat squarely on the chair, repeat
turning the other way. 5 times.
iii Lean forward to put the head on the knees. 5 times.

Note   Do not do this exercise if it causes giddiness.

Pelvic floor muscles   Exercises suitable for incontinence, or leaking from the bladder (see chapter 10).
(a) Sitting on a chair.
    i   Sit very squarely on the buttocks, squeeze the buttocks together and at the same time pull up 'underneath' as if trying to prevent oneself from going to the lavatory. It is a tiny movement but can be felt if it is being done correctly. Repeat 20 times. Once this exercise has been mastered it can be performed standing or lying and so could be done while washing up or resting in bed.

Breathing   Exercises suitable for all old people but particularly those with bronchitis, Parkinson's Disease, rheumatoid arthritis, circulatory disturbances and coldness of the hands and feet, and the bedfast.
(a) Sitting in a comfortable chair or half lying on the bed. The back should be supported in a straight position.
    i   With the hands on the lower ribs push the ribs *out* as the breath is drawn *in*. Breathe out fully but without force. 5 times.
    ii   With the hands on the stomach between the ribs, push the stomach *out* as the breath is drawn *in*. Relax and breathe out fully, letting the stomach sink down. 5 times.

Note   All breathing exercises should be done slowly. Taking deep breaths too quickly causes giddiness. The number I have indicated is only a guide as people's breathing capacities are so different; the exercises should be done in short periods with rests in between. The breathing should also be practised in other positions and during activity.

15 Outside services

Introduction The services offered in each area vary greatly, and there is wide discrepancy as to which social organisation is responsible for what service. The local Social Services Department should know whom to contact. In normal circumstances services are arranged through, or with, the authority of the doctor or hospital consultant, but in emergencies the service is provided first and the doctor consulted afterwards. There is an excellent booklet called *An ABC of Services and General Information for Disabled People* (see the list of publications at the end of this book).

Services

Social Services

Home Helps
Meals on Wheels
Chiropody
Laundry services
Day or night sitters
Hearing aids
Adaptations to the home
Telephones, television and radio

Transport to social clubs and classes run by the Social Services
Handicraft and art classes
Luncheon clubs
Sheltered workshops
Travel concessions on British Rail, local bus services, and BEA
Outings
Holidays
Residential care

Area Health Authority

District Nurses

Health Visitors

Red Cross

Nursing aid services (arranged through the district nurse)
Help with bathing, bed-changing, etc.
Medical loans: bedpans, walking frames, wheel chairs, etc.
Aids and gadgets; instructions for making them. Many are available on loan
Meals on Wheels

Invalid food
Chiropody
Shopping, changing library books, collecting pensions, etc.
Visits to the housebound and lonely
Transport to clinics and visiting relatives in hospital
Escort service for journeys on public transport
Holidays and outings

Age Concern and WRVS (Women's Royal Voluntary Service)	Meals on Wheels Welfare food: orange juice, cod liver oil, dried milk, Complan, Marmite, Bovril, Ovaltine and Horlicks at reduced rates Chiropody Secondhand clothes Seeds and seed potatoes at reduced rates Transport for hospital visiting and clinics	Escorts for long journeys Visits to the housebound and lonely Shopping, changing library books, etc. Outings Darby and Joan or Evergreen clubs Bell alarm systems installed (in some areas only) Decorating
Clubs	Darby and Joan or Evergreen: WRVS or Age Concern Luncheon clubs: Age Concern or Social Services Social clubs: Red Cross or Social Services	Clubs for the disabled: Red Cross or Social Services Art and craft classes: Red Cross or Social Services Day centres: Social Services Sheltered workshops: Social Services
Help at local level	Red Cross WRVS Age Concern Young Wives Good Neighbours	Local church organisations Local schools Youth clubs Salvation Army Citizens Advice Bureau Task Force: London Area only

Help at national level   *Age Concern,* 60 Pitcairn Road, Mitcham. Information on all voluntary services available to the elderly
British Association of the Hard of Hearing, Briarfield, Syke Ings, Iver, Bucks. Organises clubs, and gives information and advice
Help the Aged, 8–10 Denman Street, London, W1A 2AP. Information concerning the elderly
National Citizens Advice Bureau, 26 Bedford Square, London, WC1.
Royal National Institute for the Blind (RNIB), 224 Great Portland Street, London, W1. Supplies large print books (though these are usually available from the local library), braille books on free loan, talking books (for the registered blind) from The

British Talking Book Service for the Blind, Nuffield Library, Mount Pleasant, Wembley, Middlesex. These are books recorded on tape which are provided with a tape recorder for a small rental (which in some cases may be paid by the Local Authority). Application forms are available from the Social Services. The British Wireless for the Blind Fund provides a radio on free loan (apply through the Social Services). The RNIB provides aids and appliances at reduced rates. Cheap travel for the blind is sometimes available on British Rail, local buses and BEA. (Apply through the Social Services.)

Samaritans. Voluntary workers who aim to help anyone in trouble who contacts them, either personally or by telephone. They receive calls from anyone about anything, in strictest confidence, whether it is a young person taking drugs or an elderly person who is lonely and needs 'befriending'. There is a branch in most large towns, which is open all day, and many are open all night as well, including Sundays and Bank Holidays. The telephone number is in the local directory or can be obtained from the operator.

Note   Although some services ask for a small contribution based on a means test there should never be any worry about the financial side of seeking outside help. Only those who can afford it pay anything, the others are subsidised completely, making the service free (see Explanation of services, below).

Explanation of services

Home Helps   Officially employed to do housework only, and are not expected to do nursing duties. They do everyday things an old person cannot manage such as cleaning out fires and carrying coal, as well as preparing a meal for later in the day. The number of visits a week depends on the need of the client and the availability of home helps in the area. Those who can afford it pay towards the cost, those who cannot get the service free.

Meals on Wheels   Provided for a small charge if it can be afforded, otherwise they are free. The number of meals a week depends on the area, but it is usually two or three. The meal is brought ready to eat, in a heated container.

Chiropody   Undertaken at a clinic, in which case transport is arranged, or if the old person is not fit to travel, the chiropodist will visit the home. All old people should see a chiropodist regularly every six weeks or so.

Laundry services   Only for people with an incontinent person in the house. The sheets are collected regularly and replaced by clean ones; some areas will also lend sheets as a good number are required. Incontinence pads are also available, but these are disposable and burnt after use.

Day or night sitters   Available in a few areas and enable tied families to go out occasionally.

Hearing aids   Loaned with a free supply of batteries. After attendance at a special clinic, for which transport will be arranged, the doctor will fit a suitable aid if necessary.

Adaptations to the home   Mainly the installation of bars and rails by steps, a double banister, slopes over steps and hand grips by the bath and lavatory. The health visitor or social services' occupational therapist will assess the extra help that is needed, but she can be helped a great deal if she is told of any particular difficulties the elderly person has.

Telephone, television and radio   Can be installed at the discretion of the Social Services, but they are more likely to agree in rural areas than in cities, particularly if a house is isolated. The cost of installation and the rental are paid but not the calls. The Social Services can also help in paying the television licence but, again, this is more likely in rural areas.

Transport   Provided either by the ambulance service or hospital car service to all clinics, clubs and classes.

Luncheon clubs   For people who do not qualify for Meals on Wheels but who would like a good meal occasionally, combined with the social contact. A small charge is levied and transport is available to most of them. It is good for all elderly people to get out to something like this most weeks.

Day centres   Open at various times depending on the place; some are only open two or three times a week, and others every day. The range of activities they provide also varies widely; some are purely social and others run a variety of recreational classes.

Sheltered workshops   Enable many fit elderly people to continue doing light work in a supervised centre. The most usual types of work are sewing, addressing envelopes, preparing dressings for hospitals, etc.

District Nurses   Called in by the doctor to help with heavy nursing, or for the administration of injections and the changing of dressings.

The Health Visitor — Knows what help is available in her area, and will visit the home to assess what alterations are necessary, arrange Meals on Wheels, Home Helps and other services.

Nursing aid services — Usually attached to the Red Cross and are called in by the district nurse to assist with heavy lifting, bed-changing and bathing.

Medical loan — Services are run by the Red Cross or the Area Health Authority. They have various equipment for the handicapped and bedfast. They will lend bedpans, commodes, wheel-chairs and other items, but each area's stock will be a bit different so it is necessary to enquire about the more unusual items. These loans are not usually for long-term cases, but provide help when a disabled relative comes to stay or to tide over in an emergency. The length of time each area will lend equipment depends on the demand.

Aids and gadgets — Can be borrowed, and instructions on how to make many of them obtained from the Red Cross. Again, the variety and length of loan will depend on the area.

Escorts — Provided for the disabled or blind when undertaking a long journey; perhaps to visit a daughter, or to a specialised hospital for treatment.

Holidays — Usually for one or two weeks' duration, these are arranged by the Red Cross, WRVS, or the Social Services. They are primarily for people who cannot get away on their own or who live alone and rarely see anyone. They are also often used if younger relatives are ill, or wanting to go on holiday themselves, or even just to give them a rest from constant nursing and attention. As with other services, those who can, pay a little towards the cost. Transport is arranged, and escorts if necessary.

Secondhand clothes — Available from the local WRVS office for those who cannot afford an expensive item such as a warm winter coat. They will not kit people out with a new wardrobe, but provide essential articles to those who really need them. All the clothes are in excellent condition.

Outings — Run by a variety of voluntary bodies as well as the Social Services, and are usually arranged at social or luncheon clubs, or the Darby and Joan.

Darby and Joan and Evergreen Clubs Social clubs for the over sixties run by the WRVS. They normally meet weekly. There are clubs of this type even in small villages, offering tea and a chat, and usually some entertainment in the form of a film or talk.

Bell alarm systems Installed in the houses of the elderly living alone in some areas. A bell is placed in accessible positions in several rooms which rings another bell outside the house to attract attention.

If there are any difficulties at home, or ways in which help is needed, relatives should contact the Social Services and find out what can be done. Not all areas will have the variety of help I have listed, but some may have even more, so it is well worth asking.

Similarly with financial aid; if a crisis arises, such as a large unexpected bill, the Social Security will help pensioners find out all the benefits they may be entitled to.

Financial help

Pensions and Social Security Many people who need help, aids or home alterations may need extra money too, and there are thousands of old people entitled to claim from the Social Security for a variety of allowances.

Everybody over 65 years old receives a pension, and if not they should apply. If the income of an individual or married couple is below a certain level a supplementary pension can be claimed; whether one is entitled to this depends on a variety of factors and many people could claim who do not. It is well worth all pensioners finding out if they are able to claim supplementary pension because it entitles them to help with many other expenses as well.

Old people often do not like the idea of being subsidised by the State and feel that the questions asked about their means are a gross invasion of their privacy and an insult to their pride. All that is involved is a confidential interview with an officer from the Social Security, which can be carried out at home if preferred. As far as the officer is concerned it is an impersonal meeting at which he needs to find out about the income and expenditure in order to assess how much extra pension the person may be entitled to. He is not in the least interested from a personal or nosy point of view. Either get a form from the Post Office or go straight to the Social Security Office.

Other allowances

Attendance allowance   Payable to people who need full day- or night-time attendance, e.g. the incontinent or bedfast, or those who are mentally unstable and need full-time supervision to prevent injury to themselves or others. The situation must have been running for six months before a claim can be made.

Rent and rate rebates   If already on supplementary pension rent and rates are automatically paid; if not rebates must be applied for.

Glasses, and dental treatment   If on supplementary pension show the pension book to the optician or dentist and he will fill in the appropriate form for free treatment. Other people must apply for help from the Social Security Office.

Decorating   If repairs to the house or essential decorating need doing and the owner is unable to afford it, an inspector from the Social Security will assess the cost and help to pay for materials. The local Youth Club, or Task Force group (London only) will be able to help with the actual work.

Prescription charges   Everyone who draws a pension is exempt from prescription charges; the prescription just has to be signed on the back before presenting it to the chemist.

Registration of disablement   People who are severely handicapped or blind should get themselves registered with the Social Services as disabled. There are no disadvantages and many advantages. More financial help can be claimed, travel is often cheaper and a car badge enables a car to be parked to allow easy access to shops.

16 Aids and gadgets

Introduction I have chosen aids and gadgets which are simple to use and readily available or easy to make. Although every form of help should be provided for those who need it, do not rush in too early. For example, furnishing stroke victims immediately with all the artificial help they appear to need can retard recovery by never giving them the chance to rehabilitate themselves. Very few stroke victims can lift their hand to their mouth to feed themselves for some time, and it is only by persistently trying, for up to a year, that it is eventually possible. If the cutlery is altered by the addition of curves and long handles before it has been established that recovery will not take place, the movement will not be regained anyway, as no effort has been made to lift the arm. Ask for advice from the doctor about when to introduce aids.

Many home-made aids are simply adaptations of familiar articles and are easily put into use, but some are more complicated, though they are certainly not beyond the scope of the average handyman. It may be difficult for some people to get articles made, so whenever possible I have included the names of firms or shops where they are available. The larger aids such as walking aids and chairs can be borrowed, but some people will want to purchase their own, and I have recommended well-known firms who supply hospitals and the Social Services. The general public are not aware that much of this equipment is even made, let alone where to buy it. All the firms I have been in contact with have been very helpful and are willing to answer enquiries from the public, but I must stress that if a piece of equipment is ordered and found to be unsuitable it should be sent straight back. By law the firm must accept the goods and refund the money; no reason has to be given why the purchaser is not satisfied.

There are advertisements for some forms of equipment for the elderly in the popular press which are usually cheaper than those I have included, but although I am sure some of them are excellent, many are cheaply produced and some are unsafe, so be cautious.

Manufacturers' addresses are given at the end of this chapter (see also chapter 15).

Getting about, and aids to independence *Walking aid*   Red Cross (loan), Day's Medical Aids, Social Services
This gives support and helps balance. Some are available with wheels on the front legs which saves lifting. They are also made with a tray fitted on the front which allows things to be carried about. If using the tray type it is more satisfactory to

have wheels as well so that cups of tea and drinks are not spilled, and the extra weight does not have to be lifted.

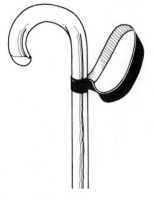

Sticks and crutches Hospital, Red Cross (loan), Boots, Social Services
It is better to get these issued by the hospital to ensure the most suitable type is used, and that they are the correct height.

Wrist strap Home-made
A piece of tape tied around the stick can be hung on the wrist while walking upstairs.

Wrist strap

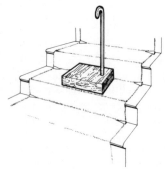

Half step with walking stick

Half step with walking stick Home-made
This is to make the size of a step smaller for those who find their stairs too deep. Use a strong wooden box and attach the stick to it. The box should be half the height of the step and narrow enough to be placed firmly on it, not overlapping it at all. The lighter the box the better as it has to be lifted up each step.

Wheel-chairs Red Cross (loan)
Wheel-chairs should only be used as a last resort. For people with strokes one-handed chairs are available, but make sure the propelling wheels are on the correct side (see Useful Books and Booklets).

Kitchen chair trolley

Kitchen chair trolley Home-made
Castors put on the legs of an upright chair give support while enabling articles to be carried on the seat.

Slope

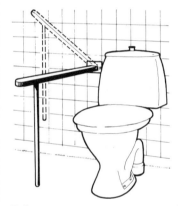

Rail support

Tip-up chair

Slope   Home-made, Social Services
A wooden slope is easier for some people than a step.

Rail by steps   Homecraft Supplies Ltd, Social Services
A wooden rail placed by the front door, or by inside steps, prevents many accidents.

Double banister   Home-made, Social Services
If at all possible there should be a banister on both sides of the stairs, even a taut piece of rope is better than nothing.

Rail support   Renray Products (UK) Ltd
This rail is attached to the wall by a hinge and can be folded away when not in use. Very useful in a small bathroom or lavatory, and by steps and bed.

Tip-up chair   John Hayes & Partners
This chair has springs attached to the seat which raises it up when the weight is leaned forward to get up. It is a high chair and good for those with arthritis of the hips, though it is fairly expensive.

Tip-up seat

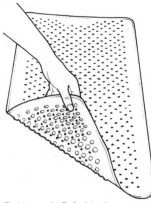

Rubbermaid Safeti bath mat

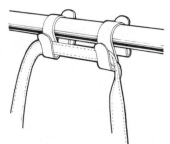

Pram clips

Tip-up seat   Carters (J.A.) Ltd
This is similar to the sprung chair but is a separate seat which can be placed in any chair.

Rubbermaid Safeti bath mat   Stores, chemists
This mat has tiny suckers on the underside to prevent slipping. It is ideal in the bath, or on the floor anywhere the feet are likely to slip. It also can be cut up to make non-slip surfaces on tables, trays etc.

Nylon shoulder bag   Stores
Light, and useful for carrying things while leaving the hands free to use an aid or sticks. It can also be clipped onto the front of a walking aid.

Pram clips   Stores
These hooks will hang over the walking aid to hold a shopping basket.

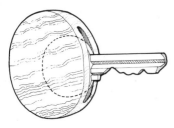

Key enlargement

Apron with pockets   Home-made
Also for carrying articles about.

Key enlargement   Home-made
Fix the key into a block of wood or large cork. It makes turning the key much easier for arthritic hands.

Lever door handles   Woolworth's, Ironmongers
Much easier than the turning type and can be worked with the elbow.

Lever handle with stirrup

Lever handle with stirrup   Home-made
For those who cannot use the lever handle with either hand or elbow. A piece of cord is attached to a bicycle pedal, or stirrup and tied to the handle, the lever handle can then be depressed and the door opened by using the foot.

General ideas

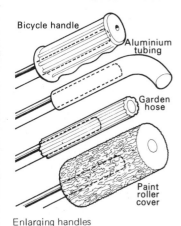

Bicycle handle
Aluminium tubing
Garden hose
Paint roller cover

Enlarging handles

Enlarging handles   Home-made, Jackel & Co. Ltd
Use bicycle handle grips, a piece of garden hose, aluminium tubing (which can be bent), sorbo rubber or a replacement paint roller cover.

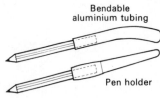

Bendable
aluminium tubing

Pen holder

Lengthening handles

Lengthening handles   Home-made
Aluminium tubing, wooden dowelling, a pen holder.

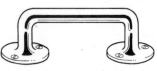

Grab handles

Grab handles Home-made, Homecraft Supplies Ltd and
Social Services
Small rails for use by lavatory, bath, chair, bed, steps etc.

Non-slip surfaces   Chemists, Woolworth's
The Rubbermaid bath mat can be cut up into required sizes to
hold plates on the table, or prevent crockery slipping while
drying up. There are many more suction cups on this make
and it therefore holds more firmly. Also use thin foam rubber
or the rubber off a ping-pong bat.

Double-suction cup

Double-suction cups   Big hardware stores, Grundy's (Rubber)
Ltd
One side of the cup is attached to a table or firm surface, the
other cup to the article to be held. Some have suction pads on
both sides, and some have to be screwed onto the article.

Language tags

Language tags   Home-made
After a stroke many people cannot express their needs. This is
greatly helped by making a series of cardboard tags with all the
necessary words on them. Include general remarks as well to
relieve some of the isolation of not being able to communicate. Suggested list: 'drink', 'hungry', 'bottle', 'bedpan', 'lie
down', 'get up', 'wash', 'pillows uncomfortable', 'glasses',
'paper', 'I cannot reach . . .', 'Turn off the light', 'Go away
please', 'Stay with me please', 'I have pain in . . .', 'How are
you?', 'Where are you going?', etc.
    Many other words can be added appropriate for the particu-
lar person. Think of things he is likely to want or be worried
about. (See chapter 3, section on speech defects.)

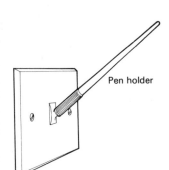

Pen holder

Switch enlargement

Switch enlargement   Home-made
Light and power switches can be lengthened by slotting an old-fashioned pen holder over the switch.

Plastic ball

Pull switch

Pull switch   Home-made
A cord pull with a plastic sports ball on the end is easier than a small switch.

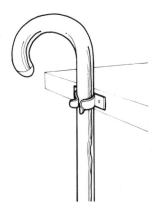

Clip for stick

Clip for stick on chair   Home-made
Screw a spring clip onto the chair to keep the stick within reach and prevent it falling about.

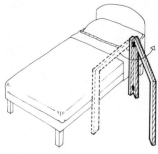

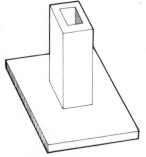

Rail by bed

Rail by the bed   Home-made, Homecraft Supplies Ltd
A wooden rail attached to the floor at right-angles to the bed
can be fitted with a swivel hinge so it can be swung round
along the side of the bed to prevent the occupant rolling out.

Blocks for bed or chair

Blocks for the chair or bed   Home-made, Homecraft Supplies
Ltd
If the height of the chair or bed needs to be raised, the legs can
be slotted into blocks which have a recess in the top to hold
them steady. If only a small raise is needed four bricks may be
used if laid flat and the legs placed in the hollow, but bricks
should not be piled up.

Monkey rope

Monkey rope   Home-made, Kimberley-Bingham & Co. Ltd
A rope attached to a hook in the ceiling makes moving about
the bed easier for some people.

Tape on glasses   Home-made
A simple enough job, but saves endless hunting for mislaid
spectacles.

Enlarged telephone dial   Army & Navy Stores
Useful for the partially sighted or those with arthritic fingers.

Helping hand   Boots, Army & Navy Stores
This ingenious gadget is like a huge pair of tongs, and enables things to be picked up off the floor without having to bend. Good for people who are giddy on bending, but should not become an excuse to sit in a chair and reach everything without getting up. They are made in different weights; an arthritic should have the very lightest one.

Helping hand

Feet steady

Feet steady   Home-made, Social Services
Nail a thin wooden batten to the floor in front of the lavatory to stop the feet slipping. It should not be too big or it will be tripped over. Alternatively use a Rubbermaid mat.

Shooting stick   Stores
Useful for active people who just need to take the weight off their feet occasionally. Better for country people as you cannot stick the spike through the pavement.

Duvet   Stores
These voluminous continental quilts are very warm and light, and save having to make the bed and lift heavy blankets.

Shavrin Levatap   Kimberley-Bingham & Co. Ltd
This lever-type tap is specifically designed for those who have arthritis in their hands and have difficulty with a normal tap fitting. It has three main features: it cannot be turned tight by people with normal hands, it only needs a quarter turn to be fully open, and it can be fitted very easily to the ordinary standard tap.

Levatap

Velcro   Haberdashery departments
See *Dressing Aids.*

Eating aids

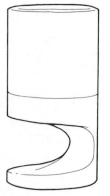

Knife and fork combined

Knife and fork combined   Carters
Useful for the one-handed. Cut with the knife edge, eat with
the fork edge; Nelson knife, or use a cheese knife.

Unspillable beaker   Chemists
Saves accidents if hands are weak.

Manoy mug

Manoy mug   Antiference Ltd, good chemists
This mug is specially designed for use by people with arthritic
hands.

Shaped spoon and fork

Shaped spoon and fork   Chemists, baby shops, Antiference
Ltd
There are several different makes of shaped cutlery which facilitate reaching the mouth. Tommee Tippee make small plastic
cutlery which is cheap, and Manoy do a beautifully designed
set for arthritics, but they are fairly expensive. Ordinary cheap
spoons and forks can be bent too.

Cutlery grip

Cutlery grip   Home-made
Screw or stick a large size cupboard handle on to the fork and spoon.

Large-handled cutlery   Home-made
Enlarge handle by using a piece of garden hose, or tying foam rubber round the handle or by pushing into a bicycle handle (see enlarging handles p. 123).

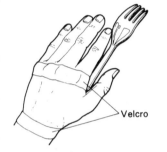

Velcro

No-grip cutlery

No-grip cutlery   Masters & Sons Ltd, Home-made
Lengthen the handles of a spoon and fork and bend them to facilitate reaching the mouth. For each implement take two strips of velcro long enough to go round the hand and wrist. Cut the velcro in half and join one hooked piece end to end with one furry piece. The velcro is put round the knuckles and another piece round the wrist to hold the cutlery in the hand.

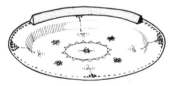

Plate guard

Plate grips   Carters, Red Cross (loan)
Use foam rubber, a ping-pong bat rubber, or a piece of Rubbermaid mat.

Plate guard   Carters, Red Cross (loan)
This attaches to the edge of the plate to prevent spills.

Suction cup

Suction egg cup

Suction egg cup   Home-made, Army & Navy Stores Ltd
Good for the one-handed. Screw suction cup to base of egg cup.

Kitchen aids

Wall can opener   Stores
If possible this should be placed where the tin can drop half an inch on to a surface below. Some have a magnetic holder which takes the lid right off which is much easier to use.

Potato peeler   Stores
'Nutbrown' make a peeler for one-handed use, it is rather like a cheese grater.

Grater   Home-made
Fix two pieces of wood together at a right angle, and put two small hooks near the top of the upright piece. Make holes at the top of the grater and put over the hooks; a plate can be put underneath to catch the grated cheese.

Grater

Slip-board   Home-made
A slab of wood has a piece of dowelling fixed across the end on the under side and two pieces in a V on the top side. The underneath one stops the board slipping from the edge of the table and the V prevents things slipping off the board. It can be used for buttering bread, steadying a bowl, or preventing things from slithering about on the table.

Slip-board

One-handed whisk   Stores
This works by an up and down action.

Rustless nails
(pointed ends up)

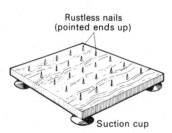

Spike-board   Home-made
Bang several rust-proof nails through a half-inch thick piece of wood. The spikes hold potatoes and vegetables steady while being peeled. It can be held steady by using either suction cups or a non-slip surface.

Suction cup

Spike-board

Non-slip tray   Big stores, Home-made
Articles on this tray will not slip off until it is tipped beyond forty-five degrees. An ordinary tray can be covered with a non-slip surface.

One-handed tray

Non-slip surface

Spring

Teapot pourer

One-handed tray   Doherty Medical, some stores, Home-made
This has a stirrup handle; two pieces of flexible wood or cane are attached at each end of the tray, and held together in the middle. It is well balanced and very useful for carrying while using a stick.

Milk saver   Stores
Small round glass object in the pan prevents the milk boiling over and saves a lot of clearing up.

Draining rack   Stores
A good sized draining rack saves having to dry up.

Teapot pourer   Home-made, Red Cross (loan)
The simplest type of pourer is to have a block of wood two inches thick, and the pot can be rested on it and tipped over the edge. A more sophisticated type for people who cannot even tilt the pot is fairly simple to make. Take two six-inch squares of wood, one one-inch thick and one half-an-inch thick. Hinge them together on one side. Buy two springs and attach them in between the wooden squares on the opposite side from the hinges. Nail a thin dowel across the top piece on the hinged side to stop the pot slipping, and a clip the opposite side to prevent it popping up when not wanted. It works on the same principle as the tip-up chair.

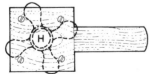

Tap turner

Tap turner   Home-made, Red Cross (loan)
Many arthritics have trouble turning taps on and off, and this is a cheaper way of easing the situation than altering the taps. Take a two-inch square piece of wood, screw four screws through it in a circle. Cover each one with a small piece of rubber or plastic tubing. Nail a handle one inch wide by six inches long to the square. The screws are fitted between the spokes of the tap and the handle used as a lever to turn the tap on.

Clip-on apron

Pan guard

Lever taps   Hardware Stores
Lever taps are easier to use than the old fashioned type, and can be worked by the elbow, but they tend to get stiff, and ordinary hands can turn them off very tightly.

Strainer spoon   Hardware Stores
This large spoon is full of holes and enables vegetables to be drained as they are removed from the pan, rather than having to lift a heavy saucepan full of water.

Clip-on apron   Home-made
Cut off the strings, and turn the waist band down. Thread a piece of stiff wire through the band, it can then be clipped on and will grip round the waist.

Brexton insulated food bag   Large stores, Boots
This specially designed bag keeps food hot, or cold, for up to four hours. It is useful when meals are prepared in advance. It is fairly expensive but is ideal for picnics as well.

Thermos   Stores, Chemists
For those who cannot make themselves a drink, it can be made in advance and kept hot until wanted.

Pan guard   Crayleigh Safeguard Products, Gas & Electricity Boards, Mothercare
A very important safety device to avoid burns and scalds. The guard is fixed to the top of the stove, and some have slots to take the saucepan handles.

Kennroy auto tea caddy   Stores
This tea dispenser is fixed to the wall, and has a push button which releases one teaspoonful of tea at a time. Saves struggling with tins.

Tea infuser   Stores
A double-sided perforated teaspoon for making single cups of tea without a pot. The tea is enclosed in the spoon and the water poured over it in the cup.

Foam mat on draining board   Woolworth's
Prevents breakages from crockery slipping out of weak hands.

Swivel chair   Furniture shops, Office suppliers
If the kitchen is small and compact a swivel chair saves a lot of

moving around, and is particularly useful for those who feel giddy when turning round.

Hot water bottle holder

Hot water bottle holder   Home-made
Many burns are caused when hot bottles are being filled. Cut an inch-wide piece out of a block of wood six inches by four, and attach it to the wall, preferably near the kettle. The neck of the bottle is held by the slot in the wood. Also use a funnel.

'Undo-it' jar opener

'Undo-it' jar opener   Army & Navy Stores
This gadget is a V-shaped piece of serrated metal which is attached to the under surface of a table or wall cupboard. The serrations hold the lid, leaving two hands free to turn the jar.

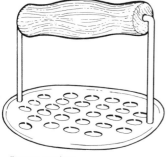

Potato masher

Potato masher   Stores, Army & Navy Stores
The D-shaped handle of this masher is easier than the conventional type.

Saucepan lids

Saucepan lids   Home-made
Most knobs are attached by a screw which can be undone, and
a large wooden knob or cotton reel put in its place. Useful also
for the kettle and teapot.

Wood on jar lid

Jar lids   Home-made
Jar lids that are difficult to grip and turn can have a square
block of wood screwed on to the top which gives a firmer
hold.

Long-handled brush and pan   D. G. Hazelock
Good for people with arthritic hips or who are giddy on bending.

Toilet aids

Rail by lavatory

Rail by the lavatory   Home-made, Homecraft Supplies Ltd,
Social Services
If the toilet is narrow enough two handles can be fixed to the
wall, one each side, to help when getting up.

Toilet seat raise

Toilet seat raise   Homecraft Supplies Ltd, Red Cross (loan)
This raises the seat to make getting up easier. They are made in different heights.

Tip-up toilet seat

Tip-up toilet seat   John Hayes & Partners
This seat is similar to the tip-up chair and has a spring loaded seat which raises the person up as she leans forward to get up.

Rubbermaid Safeti mat   Chemists, Stores
A rubber mat in front of the lavatory prevents the feet slipping.

Toilet tongs

Toilet tongs   Home-made, Red Cross (loan)
A pair of kitchen tongs can be used to hold paper or other cleansing material, and makes reaching much easier.

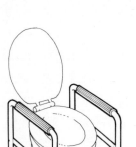

Toilet aid

Dressing aids

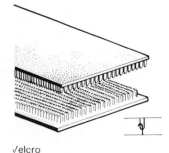

Velcro

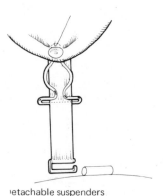

etachable suspenders

Toilet aid 'Seaco'   Medico-Therapeutics Ltd
This support round the lavatory seat is made of tubular steel
and is attached to the floor. It gives firm support while getting
on or off the lavatory.

The Disabled Living Foundation have produced a booklet
showing alterations and instructions to make dressing easier
for the handicapped. It is called *How to Adapt Existing Clothing for the Disabled* and costs 50p.

Velcro   Haberdashery departments
This double-sided tape has two surfaces which stick firmly
together, and can be peeled apart. It is very strong and can be
used instead of zips, buttons, hooks and poppers. Use on
trousers, ties, cuffs, bras, shirts, etc.

Clothes pegs
Attach pants to trousers and pull the two up together.

Detachable suspenders   Stores
Keep the suspenders attached to the stocking, and when
dressing hook the suspender onto the belt by using a loop over
a button, or if it has a bar attachment, slip that through a loop
on the belt.

Hold-up stockings   Stores
These have a garter incorporated in the stocking and need no suspenders. They should not be used by people with bad circulation in the legs, or who have ulcers and varicose veins.

Pantigirdle   Stores, Marks & Spencer
Elasticated pants which act as a corset, and are easier to put on. Some have detachable suspenders.

Stocking gutter   Home-made, Carters (J.S.) Ltd, Red Cross
Sew two suspenders on to a piece of cardboard or a rubber floor tile about seven inches by nine. On to the other end sew the ends of a piece of tape two yards long. The stocking is threaded over the cardboard and attached to the suspenders. The gutter is then thrown on to the floor, while keeping hold of the tape, the foot placed in the stocking and the whole thing pulled up by the tape. As soon as it is high enough to be reached the gutter can be removed and the stocking pulled up the rest of the way. Very good for those with arthritis in the hips.

Stocking gutter

Front-opening bra   Stores, Mothercare
Much easier to put on than the back opening type. The front hooks can be replaced by velcro.

Button-through skirts and dresses   Stores, Home alterations
Much easier to put on than having to struggle with putting clothes over the head. Also avoids having to stand up while dressing.

Loops on socks

Loops on socks   Home-made
Sew tape loops on to socks which can be pulled up by a hooked stick. Also use stocking gutter.

Long-handled shoe horn   Home-made, Carters (J.A.) Ltd
Attach a long handle to an ordinary shoe horn.

Kiwi elastic laces   Some large shoe shops, Homecraft Supplies Ltd
These laces can remain tied up and the foot slipped into the shoe. They are made in various lengths, in black and brown.

No-tie tie

Clip-on tie

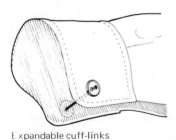

E xpandable cuff-links

No-tie tie   Home-made
Cut the back piece out of a made up tie and replace it with elastic. The tie can just be slipped over the head without undoing the knot.

Clip-on tie   Home-made, Stores
Cut out the back of a made up tie and sew a curtain hook on to the knot which can be attached to the front of the shirt collar.

Expanding cuff-links   Home-made
Connect cuff-links, or two buttons with shearing elastic, or sew the ordinary button on with shearing elastic to allow the cuff to expand as the hand is pushed through. Good for people with strokes.

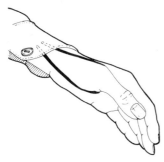

Loops on cuffs

Loops on cuffs   Home-made
Sew elastic loops onto the cuffs of shirts and sweaters. The loop is hooked over the thumb while putting on a jacket or coat to keep the sleeve down.

Clip-on braces   Woolworth's, Stores
This avoids having to do up buttons, and can be done with one hand.

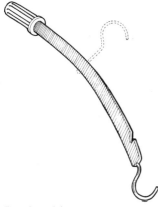

Dressing stick

Dressing stick   Home-made
Remove the hook from a wooden coat hanger, and screw the hook into the end of the hanger. Very useful for pulling on socks and stockings, or lifting a coat off the shoulder. The handle may need enlarging for some people.

Magnifying mirror   Stores
Useful for making up or shaving. They are usually on a stand.

Hair brush holder

Hair brush holder   Home-made
Put a wide elastic band round the back of a man's hair brush. The hand can be slipped through to give a firm hold.

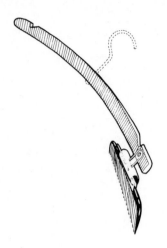

Long-handled comb

Long-handled comb   Home-made
Using a wooden coat hanger with the hook removed, screw a bulldog clip (stationers) at right-angles to the end of it. Put the comb in the clip at the appropriate angle.

Non-slip soles   Cobblers
All leather soled shoes should have non-slip soles stuck onto them.

Odd-sized shoes
Many people with bunions or swelling in one foot need odd sized shoes, and they can be obtained from the Managing Director of Dolcis, 7–13 Dover Street, London, SE1.

Shoes
The most suitable shoes for elderly women are a make called 'Diana Broadway', and they are available from most good shoe shops.

Washing and bathing aids

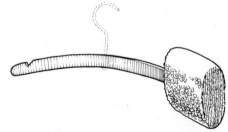

Sponge on handle

Sponge on handle   Home-made
Make a hole in the sponge and stick it on to the end of a wooden clothes hanger or suitable piece of wood. If the handle is too narrow, enlarge it with sorbo rubber or a bicycle handle.

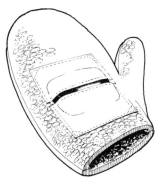

Soap glove mit

Toe washer

Suction nail brush

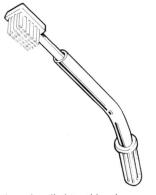

Long-handled toothbrush

Soap glove mit   Home-made
Make a mitten of foam rubber, and attach a pocket to the palm in which to put the soap.

Toe washer   Home-made, Red Cross (loan)
Buy a plastic fly swat from Woolworth's, and cover it with thin foam or a flannel. This facilitates washing the feet and between the toes.

Suction nail brush   Home-made
Attach two double-suction cups to the back of a nail brush. It is stuck to the basin, bristles up, and is good for people with one hand.

Long-handled toothbrush   Home-made
Push a piece of curved aluminium tubing on to the brush. Otherwise use a wooden coat hanger.

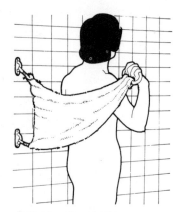

Roller towel on elastic

Long-handled razor   Home-made
Directions as for the toothbrush.

Battery electric shaver   Boots, Electrical shops
Safer, easier and quicker than a 'scraper'.

Rubber hose hair washer   Chemists
Useful for bathing and hair washing.

Roller towel on elastic   Home-made, Red Cross (loan)
Sew nine-inch pieces of elastic on to one end of the towel, and attach to the door. It only has to be pulled one way to dry the back.

Rubbermaid Safeti mat   Chemists
Use one in the bath, and one on the floor. A piece can be cut off one and stuck to the edge of the bath to make a non-slip hand grip.

Bath safety rails   Homecraft   Supplies,   Hardware   Stores, Home-made
Hand rails can be attached to the wall and the edge of the bath.

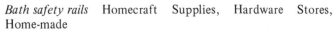

'Economic' bath safety rail   Kimberley-Bingham & Co. Ltd
This rail fits any bath with conventional taps and hinges up over the end of the bath when not in use.

'Economic' safety rail

Safety rail   Carters (J.A.) Ltd
This is a simpler version of the above and is attached to the wall.

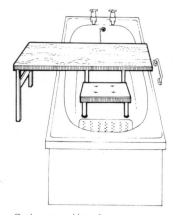

Bath seat and bench

Bath seat and bench   M. Masters & Sons, Home-made
Enables elderly people to get in and out of the bath safely. For the seat, use a four-legged stool, or buy a stool (see below) and screw single suction cups to the bottom of the legs which prevents it slipping in the bath. The bench can be made from a plank of wood supported on legs at one end. The bench is placed just behind the stool with the legs on the floor and the free end resting on the far side of the bath. Single suction cups screwed to the under side will keep it steady on the bath. The plank can be attached to the stool by vertical slats. Precautions: make sure the plank is strong enough, and that it is free from splinters. To use this combination, sit on the plank and

Bath seat

slide your seat along, lifting your legs over the edge of the bath. Move down from the bench on to the stool which can be sat on to wash. The feet should be on a rubber mat.

Bath seat   Carters (J.A.) Ltd
A seat only which is placed in the bath.

Shower   Dolphin Showers Ltd
A shower is fairly easy to install and is simpler to use than a bath. I have suggested this make because it has an anti-scald device, and keeps the water at a constant temperature.

Aids for the bedfast

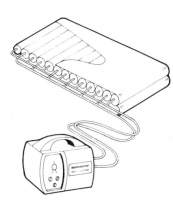

Ripple bed

Cradle   Red Cross (loan)
It is important to keep the weight of the bed clothes off the feet, to enable the feet to be moved freely to avoid sores and thromboses.

Medical sheepskin   Garroulds Ltd
These sheepskins are specially treated to make washing easy. They are good for preventing bed sores, and for the incontinent, because they absorb 33 per cent of their weight in moisture, which keeps the surface on which the patient is lying dry. They are expensive.

Ripple bed   Talley Surgical Instruments
Another very expensive item, though it can be hired. It is a polythene mattress which varies the pressure under the person, and is very efficient at preventing bed sores because no one part of the body takes the full weight for any length of time.

Heel pads   Home-made
A pair of old socks several sizes too large can be lined in the heel with thick foam rubber. They must not be too tight or they will do more harm than good. Talley Surgical Instruments also make sheepskin heel pads.

Baby intercom   Electrical shops
This two-way intercom enables an elderly person to contact someone in another room, but should not be used to have relatives running backwards and forwards.

Bedpans and bottles   Red Cross (loan)
It is always preferable for all concerned for the person to get out of bed to use a commode or the lavatory if possible. Bedpans and bottles should only be used if he or she is too ill to move.

Inflatable ring-cum-bedpan   Leyland & Birmingham Rubber Co.
This is useful just as a ring to prevent bed sores and to make the patient more comfortable. It can also be kept in place for badly incontinent people, or used as an ordinary bedpan. Care must be taken to avoid using it with people who are just lazy. It is very easy to get into the habit of using it as an easy way out, but will soon make some people incontinent, and is a possible source of infection.

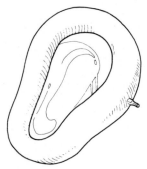
Inflatable ring-cum-bedpan

Bendable straws

Bendable straws   Boots, W. H. Smith & Sons
Straws that bend in the middle without flattening make drinking in bed much easier.

Non-spillable beaker

Non-spillable beaker   Chemists
There are various makes with or without handles that have tops and a perforated spout. Even when tipped upside down very little liquid will spill.

Pelican bib

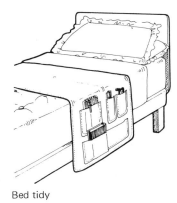

Bed tidy

Pelican bib   Chemists, Mothercare
This plastic bib has a pouch at the bottom to catch spilled food and drink.

Bed tidy   Home-made
A large piece of material spread across the bed with pockets in the hanging sides keeps belongings handy and tidy.

Rubber ring   Toy shops
A child's inflatable swimming ring can be used to keep pressure off the sacrum. Only use a rubber ring if a sorbo one cannot be borrowed from the Red Cross.

Incontinence aids   *Disposable nappies*   Chemists
Good to use with plastic pants to catch minor leaks.

Inco protective-pants   Boots
These polythene pants have popper fastenings and are used with disposable pads and liners.

Incontinence pads   Boots, Social Services
Disposable pads about two feet by eighteen inches. They have paper padding on one side and waterproofing on the other, and are very good for saving bedding and using on the seat of a chair.

Open-backed nightdress   Army & Navy Stores, Home-made
An ordinary nightdress can be opened down the back, and men can wear pyjama tops only.

Plastic sandals   Shoe shops
Washable in soap and water. Suitable for active, badly incontinent people.

Inflatable ring-cum-bedpan
See *Aids for the Bedfast.*

Sheepskin slippers   Marks & Spencer
These very warm slippers can be washed in soap and water.

Waterproof mattress cover   Boots
Protects mattress from getting wet, and can be wiped clean.

Marathon one-way dri sheet   Chemists, Marathon Knitwear
This is a non-absorbent sheet which allows moisture to pass right through it to be absorbed by the pad underneath. The sheet is left feeling dry. Very good for all incontinent people and easy to wash and dry.

Nappy cleaners   Chemists
There are many makes of nappy cleaner and they are all much the same. A small amount of powder is put in a bucket of water, and soiled linen is soaked for a minimum of two hours; it sterilises and whitens leaving the linen ready to be rinsed and dried.

Disinfectant   Chemists, Stores
Incontinence is always a potential cause of infection, and it is necessary to keep all clothes and furniture with which the patient comes into contact scrupulously clean.

Pastimes

Book rest

Book rest   Home-made, Red Cross (loan)
Either prop the book up in a cardboard box, or hinge two pieces of wood together, with a slat at the bottom of one to support the book, and a rubber band between the two to stop them sliding apart.

Page turner

Page turner   Home-made
A rubber finger stall on the end of a stick makes page turning easier for arthritic fingers.

Magnifying glass   Stores
Helpful for the partially sighted, some glasses are on a stand.

Large-print books   Library
Available at most public libraries (see chapter 15).

Needle threader   Haberdashery departments
Helps people to sew and do their own mending.

Quick unpick   Haberdashery departments
Aids failing eyes and arthritic fingers when sewing.

Card holder

Card holder   Home-made
Either stand the cards between the bristles of a scrubbing brush, or cut one side out of a cardboard box and prop the cards inside.

Enlarged pencil

Enlarged pencil   Home-made
Either push a plastic tap swirl on to the pencil, or slide it through a plastic sports ball. Some stationers sell very fat pens with several different coloured biros inside.

Electric scissors   Stores
Ordinary scissors are very difficult to use with arthritis in the hands; these take all the effort out of cutting. They run on batteries.

Knitting needle clamp   Red Cross (loan)
One needle is clamped to the arm of a chair, the other can be worked by the normal hand.

Taped books   National Listening Library
Tapes are sent by post. The Social Services may help with equipment.

Matchbox holder   Home-made
Stick the outer case to a heavy block of wood. The inside box can be replaced when it is empty.

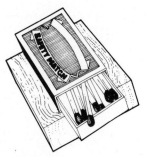

Matchbox holder

Braille telephone dial   RNIB
Enables blind people to dial without making mistakes.

Telephone flasher for the deaf
Londex Ltd, 207 Anerley Road, London, SE20.

Telephone amplifier   GPO Telephone Sales Office
A volume control is incorporated in the ear-piece of the telephone and is excellent for the hard of hearing.

Talking book machine   Social Services
Many books have been transferred on to tape, and the tape and the recorder are available, usually for a small rent. Some areas also have a talking newspaper.

Safety aids   *Whistle*   Sports shops
Put a whistle on a piece of string and wear it round the neck. If in trouble it will be heard for some way if blown hard.

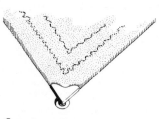

Carpet corners

Light or bell system   Social Services (some areas), Electrician, Davies Sound Control Ltd, Lakeside, Woolsington, Newcastle on Tyne, NE13 8AL
See chapter 15.

Carpet corners   Ironmonger
Keep the corners of rugs and carpets from turning up. Prevent the rugs slipping as well as keeping them flat to avoid tripping. Or, tack corners to the floor.

Fireguard   Stores, Mothercare
Always put a guard in front of the fire every single time it is lit. The large nursery type is the best and does not prevent the heat coming through as the small-meshed ones do.

Hot water bottle cover   Home-made, Stores
Always put a cover on a bottle to prevent burns, which are very common, particularly in people with defective sensation or paralysed limbs.

Ferrule   Boots, Hospital, Grundy's Rubber Co.
All walking sticks or crutches should have a rubber ferrule on the bottom. Sticks with a metal cap on the end are very dangerous.

Slip-board

Slip-board   Home-made
If possible put the cooker next to the sink and place a board between the two so that pans can be slid across on to the draining board without having to be lifted. Very useful for those with arthritis or painful shoulders, and after a fractured wrist.

Cut-out kettle   Stores
Some kettles are made with a special switch which automatically turns them off when the water is boiling. Good for the forgetful.

Automatic time switch   Electrical Shops
This clock can be set to switch on an electric blanket before going to bed; or the fire, so the house is warm on returning from an outing. It switches the appliance off after three hours. Must be well maintained.

Funnel   Stores
Use a funnel when filling a hot water bottle.

Common sense and precautions

1 Sit to wash up, peel the vegetables, and do the ironing.
2 Use sliced bread.
3 Never climb step ladders, or climb on to a chair. If something is out of reach wait until somebody comes.
4 Always use a fireguard.
5 Do not get into bed with the electric blanket on unless it is the 'over' type. For those with bad memories use an automatic time switch which will turn it off after three hours.
6 Do not use small 'slip' mats, they are very aptly named.
7 Fix unsteady wardrobes to the floor.

8 When buying new clothes, or making them, try to buy flame-proof materials if possible. If this proves difficult use those which are of low flammability such as bri-nylon, polyester, or acetate rayon. These tend to shrivel up rather than burn. Do not use cotton, or acrylic fibres such as acrilan, courtelle or orlon, which are very inflammable.

9 Do not put clocks and regularly used articles on the mantel shelf above the fire. Leaning over can catch clothes on fire or may result in a fall.

10 Use an electric razor in preference to a hand razor.

11 Do not wear garters. They are nearly always too tight and cause cold swollen feet.

12 Keep the bed and chair away from a wall radiator. Many burns are caused by the hand or leg resting on it while asleep.

13 Keep a torch by the bed, unless the light switch is readily accessible.

14 Label all medicines and throw away any not in use.

15 Keep all dark corners, stairs and steps well lit.

16 Use a kettle with an automatic cut-out switch.

17 Have a pan guard fitted on the cooker.

18 If using a stick make sure it has a rubber ferrule on the bottom.

19 A stick the wrong height can be more hazardous than going without. To measure the correct length put the arm by the side with the wrist extended and the elbow slightly bent. Someone else can measure from the palm of the hand to the floor. Wooden sticks can be sawn off at the appropriate place; metal ones are adjustable.

20 Have hand rails fitted to the wall by all steps, and near the lavatory and bath.

21 If stairs are difficult bring the bed downstairs.

22 A commode for night time (can be borrowed from the Red Cross) is useful but should not become a habit.

23 If possible have all electric plugs in constant use raised to waist height, particularly if suffering from giddiness.

24 It is expensive, but it is a good thing if a gas cooker can be replaced with an electric one. Almost 50 per cent of old people have some impairment in their sense of smell.

25 Old people feel the cold much more than the young; partly due to lack of exercise, particularly if they are disabled in some way, and partly due to a fault in their heating mechanism. They should make a conscious effort to wear adequate clothing and to keep the house warm.

The most effective and long-lasting way to keep warm is exercise. I do not mean physical jerks but just going about

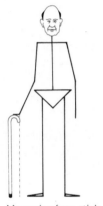

Measuring for a stick

the house and garden doing the chores and normal everyday things. Deep breathing is also a good way to encourage the circulation, and so keep warm.

26 Have the meter raised if it is near the floor.

27 A luminous strip round light switches saves groping.

28 Wear shoes, not slippers.

29 Don't have flexes trailing on the floor.

30 Adequate lighting to outside lavatories.

31 Door bolts should be at waist level.

32 Return light switch on the stairs.

33 Guard paraffin heaters from draughts, also gas cookers.

Manufacturers' addresses   Antiference Ltd, Tableware Division, Bicester Road, Aylesbury, Bucks.

Army and Navy Stores, Victoria Street, London, SW1.

British Red Cross Society, 9 Grosvenor Crescent, London, SW1.

Carters (J.A.) Ltd, 65 Wigmore Street, London, W1.

Crayleigh Safeguard Products Ltd, 92 Portland Place, London, W1.

Day's Medical Aids, Llandow Industrial Estate, Cowbridge, Glamorgan.

Disabled Living Foundation, 346 Kensington High Street, London, W14 8NS.

Doherty Medical, Eedee House, Charlton Road, Edmonton, London, N9.

Dolphin Showers Ltd, Weir Lane, Worcester.

E. R. Garroulds Ltd, 9 Hardwicks Way, Wandsworth, London, SW18.

Grundy's (Rubber) Ltd, 167 Burton Road, Withington, Manchester, H20 8LN.

D. G. Haslock, 40–48 Temple Street, Wolverhampton, WV4 4AW.

John Hayes and Partners, Lowe Edge, Wychbold, Droitwich Spa, Worcs.

Homecraft Supplies Ltd, 27 Trinity Street, London, SW17.

Jackel & Co. Ltd, Kitty Brewster Estate, Blythe, Northumberland.

Kimberley-Bingham & Co. Ltd, 44 Washington Street, Birmingham 1.

Leyland and Birmingham Rubber Co. Ltd, Harrowby Street, Cardiff.

Marathon Knitwear (Nottm) Ltd, Peveril Street, Nottingham.

M. Masters & Sons Ltd, 240 New Kent Road, London, SE1.

Medico-Therapeutics Ltd, (Technical & Research), 44 Connaught Gardens, London, N13.

Mothercare-by-Post, Cherry Tree Road, Watford WDE 5SH.
Renray Products (UK) Ltd, 75 Woodvale Road, Belfast, BT13 3BP.
Talley Surgical Instruments Ltd, 47 Theobald Street, Boreham Wood, Herts.

Glossary

Although I have tried to use as few medical terms as possible, there are several words or phrases which may need a little explanation. The definitions I have given are strictly within the context of this book and are not necessarily those found in a dictionary or used in general terms.

Abduction	Movement of a limb *away* from the mid-line of the body.
Adduction	Movement of a limb *towards* the mid-line of the body.
Adhesions	The structures of a joint become stuck together due to inflammation in the area, and cause pain and limitation of movements.
Analgesic	Pain-relieving property in some drugs such as aspirin.
Capsule	Fibrous envelope protecting a joint.
Cartilage	Flexible, smooth covering, protecting the ends of bones forming a joint. Ensures gliding movement of one bone on the other.
Deformity	Fixed deviation from the normal resulting in reduction of movement in a joint.
Extension	Straightening or stretching out of a joint.
Flaccid	Floppy, paralysed.
Flexion	Bending of a joint.
Haemorrhage	Bleeding.
Mucus	Substance produced by the lining of some internal parts of the body to act as a lubricant, and protect sensitive surfaces from damage.
Pattern of movement	Muscles working together in groups to produce normal smooth movements.
Sacrum	Triangular bone at the base of the spine.
Spasm	Unnatural tightening or contraction of muscles.
Spasticity	Abnormal patterns of movements produced by unnaturally tight muscles.
Sputum	Phlegm from the chest.
Stimulus	Thing which produces a functional reaction or movement.
Thrombosis	Clot in a blood vessel.
Tissues	The substances of which the body is made up, skin, muscle, bone, etc.
Trauma	Injury.

Some useful addresses, books and booklets

Addresses

Friends-by-Post. Penfriend service. Mrs I. Salomon, Ferring, Adlington Road, Wilmslow, Cheshire.

'*Friends of the Air*', Joint Involvement Mutual Society, White Rails, 86 Turnpike Road, Aughton, Ormskirk, Lancs. Contact by pen friends, telephone, magazines and newsletters.

Homebound Craftsman, 25a Holland Street, London, W8. This is a group that sends out knitting orders to housebound people from the general public. The wool and pattern are provided, and payment too. They also have a shop at the above address where articles made by the housebound can be sold. Mostly they have toys, wooden articles, leather work, basketry and pottery, but they will not take work unless it is of a high standard.

Jigsaw Puzzle Loan Club, c/o Miss R. Cockerton, MBE, 16 Bucks Avenue, Watford Heath, Herts. No charge.

Large Print Books. Local library or from Ulverscroft Large Print Books Ltd, Station Road, Glenfield, Leicester.

Mobile Library Service. Available in most rural areas; apply to the local branch library.

National Listening Library, 49 Great Cumberland Place, London, W1H 7LH. Tapes sent by post.

Reweaving Industry, Keswick, Cumberland. This firm sends out garments for invisible mending, and provides postal instruction.

Wider Horizons. New Membership Secretary, Laburnum Cottage, Back Street, Bridge of Earn, Perth. Magazine written by members, poems, articles, hints and correspondence group.

Books and booklets

An ABC of Services and General Information for Disabled People. Disablement Income Group, 180 Tottenham Court Road, London, W1.

Access for the Disabled. The Central Council for the Disabled, 34 Eccleston Square, London, SW1. This series of booklets is a guide to access to public places and facilities in many large towns and cities.

The Aged, Their Understanding and Care by Dr Klaus Bergman. Wolfe. Excellent on 'the problems and behaviour patterns' of old people.

All About Strokes by A. Barham Carter. Panther Science.

Consumer's Guide to the British Social Services by Phyllis Willmot. Penguin, 2nd edition.

Cooking for the Over 60s. Food Information Centre, 12 Park Lane, Croydon, Surrey.

Easy Cooking for One or Two by Louise Davies. Penguin.
Written by a dietician specially for the elderly and combines
cheapness of recipes and nourishment.
Easy Path to Gardening. The Disabled Living Foundation.
Gardening for the Elderly and Handicapped by Leslie Snook.
Pan.
Guide to Activities for Older People by Gwyneth Wallis. Elek.
From Age Concern, 60 Pitcairn Road, Mitcham.
Holiday Addresses for Chest, Heart, and 'Stroke' Patients. The
Chest and Heart Association, Tavistock House North, Tavi-
stock Square, London, WC1.
Holidays for the Physically Handicapped. The Central Council
for the Disabled, 34 Eccleston Square, London, SW1.
How to Adapt Clothing for the Disabled. The Disabled Living
Foundation.
Incontinence, Some Problems, Suggestions, and Conclusions.
The Disabled Living Foundation, 346 Kensington High Street,
London, W14 8NS.
In Touch. BBC publication. Aids and services for blind and
partially sighted people.
London for the Disabled. The Disabled Living Foundation,
346 Kensington High Street, London, W14 8NS. This is a
guide to access to shops, theatres and lavatories, as well as
places of interest.
Pins and Needles is a monthly sewing and knitting magazine
which carries advertisements for cut-price wool, material rem-
nants, and bundles of leather, patchwork, ribbon etc. The
remnants I have had have been very good value indeed.
People in Wheelchairs – Hints for Helpers. The Red Cross.
Seventy Plus, A Handbook for Easier Living for the Elderly.
BBC publication, London, W1A 1AR.
A Stroke in the Family by Valerie Eaton Griffith. Penguin.
Anybody with a friend or relative whose stroke involves
speech difficulties should have this book.
Working at Home by Joanna Johnson. The British Council for
Rehabilitation of the Disabled, Tavistock House (South), Tavi-
stock Square, London, WC1H 9LB.
Your Garden and Your Rheumatism. The Arthritis and
Rheumatism Council, Faraday House, 8 Charing Cross Road,
London, WC2.
Yours. A monthly paper issued free by Help the Aged; distri-
buted by clubs, hospitals etc.

Index